GT

A Fly Fisher's Guide to Giant Trevally

PETER McLEOD

MERLIN UNWIN BOOKS

PART I: GUIDE

PART II: DESTINATIONS

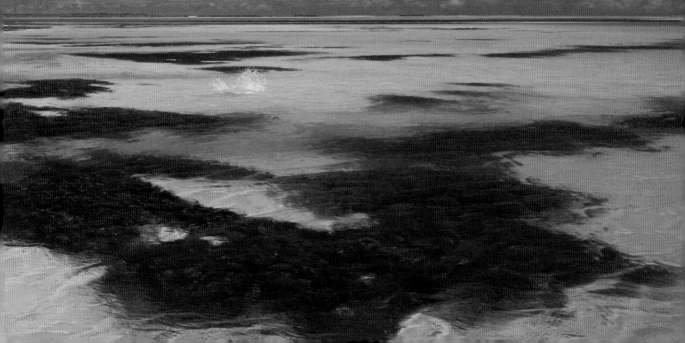

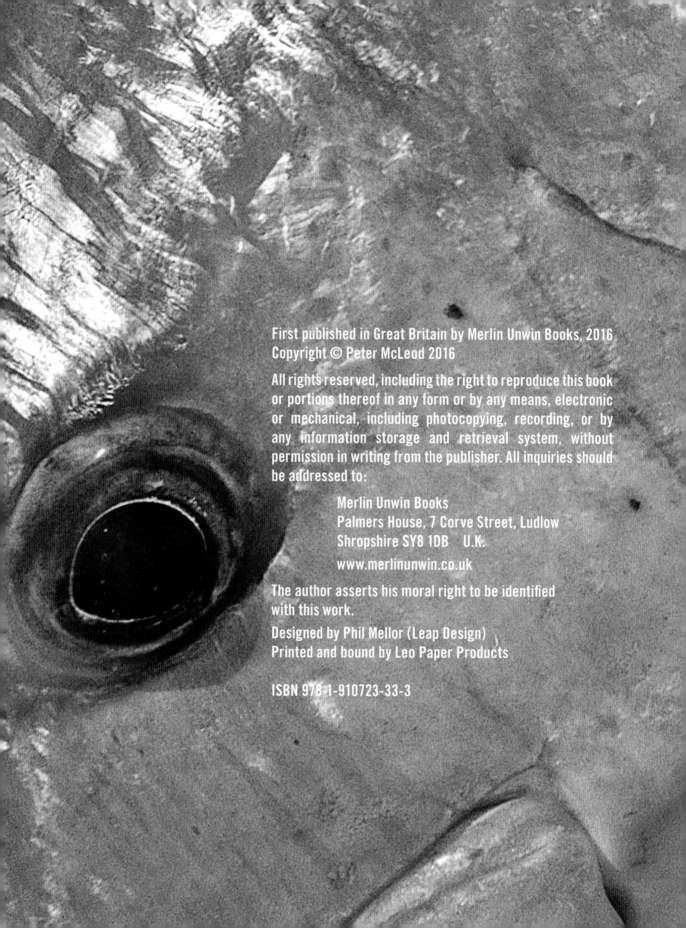

Merlin Unwin Books
Palmers House, 7 Corve Street, Ludlow
Shropshire SY8 1DB   U.K.

www.merlinunwin.co.uk

Designed by Phil Mellor (Leap Design)
Printed and bound by Leo Paper Products

ISBN 978-1-910723-33-3

ACKNOWLEDGEMENTS

When embarking on an adventure like this book, there are some driving forces that need to be recognised. Family aside for putting up with me while I worked on this, the first I would like to mention is Will Bond, sadly no longer with us. Will is responsible for my total passion for saltwater flyfishing. When I first began working as a flyfishing agent, green and wet behind the ears, it was he who took me under his wing and imparted his huge wealth of saltwater knowledge that started my passion. I am only sad that so many of the amesChristmas for his fly designs and technical insight dventures that I have experienced over the years, I could not share with him.

Although there are too many to thank, I would like to mention a few others who had particular influence on me as a fishermen and set me on this path of GT obsession. Fishing with Andrew Parsons at Benguerra in Mozambique was a baptism by fire. He taught the crucial skill to fight fish far harder with a flyrod than I ever dreamed possible; by applying the angles, the fish can be brought to the boat faster and released in better condition. Arno Mathee is one of the most modest of characters but I firmly believe he can actually think like a fish and he taught me much about habitat. Keith Rose-Innes indoctrinated me on atoll fishing, along with Serge Samson, Graeme Field, Vaughn Driessel, Paul Boyers, Simon Corrie, Teannaki Kaiboboki, Rob Scott, Mark Murray, Tim Pask and many others.

This book is very much a joint effort, a bringing together of collective knowledge. Each and every contributor to this book has had to put up with me pestering and questioning. As experts, they have ensured what has been written is not rubbish. I would like to thank Andy Danylchuk for imparting his scientific expertise, Gerhard Laubscher for his input into some of the technical sections, James Christmas for his fly designs and technical insight and Andreas Linz for his encyclopedic knowledge of saltwater patterns.

Fishing is a constantly evolving process. The views represented in this book are our opinions but I hope will prove useful. Others will have differing opinions and will experience different things. No one has all the answers, and that is fine in the ever-evolving manuscript of debate.

Will Bond (wearing blue hat)

Andrew Parsons

"When my mind visualises the pristine wilderness of the saltwater flats, there is one species that I picture marauding across them..."

PART I

GUIDE

To fish for giant trevally, first you must understand your quarry. What is it about their physical make up that allows them to be so successful? This section will guide you to a greater understanding of the species, where they like to hunt and why, how you locate them and what equipment you need to tackle them. You will discover best practices for fighting them on the fly and for releasing them unharmed.

CHAPTER 1 - THE BEGINNING

The giant trevally (GT) or *Caranx ignoblis*. This species always has the power to make me shiver with excitement. In my mind's eye I see a pack of them charge across the flats, ripping into baitfish, before surging off at a tangent, pushing water off their snouts like some kind of half-submerged nuclear submarine. In the line-up from bonefish to tarpon, GTs have captured my heart. All trevally species offer the fly angler a huge test of skill and endurance, but GTs will push your tackle to destruction. I have seen them pluck an angler's soul from his body, destroying hundreds of pounds' worth of tackle he has spent the last six months carefully researching and saving for. I have seen GTs charge out from overhanging coral, smash a fly, then eat another angler's fly before tearing out to sea dragging both lines, before cutting them both on the reef. The pièce de résistance was a client of mine who was charged by a pack of GTs on the flats on Cosmoledo. As she cast and began to strip the fly, the front fish came out of the water and bit the top four inches off her brand new Sage 12# fly rod. They are so beautifully aggressive. They are the bulldogs of the flats.

Early in my saltwater career as I fished around the Caribbean I heard tales of this mad fish species that swam in other waters, had the power of permit but were ferocious with it. Having spent a number of years with a permit obsession, the thought of chasing after a fish species that might be more inclined to actually eat a fly seemed very attractive. These fish of my dreams were to be found in the Indian Ocean and the Pacific and apparently were too powerful to land on fly. It was only later I discovered that a collective of innovative souls had been catching them on fly on the far-flung atoll of Christmas Island (Kiritimati) in the Republic of Kiribati for several decades. At that time, saltwater fishing had only just ventured across the Atlantic from the US and our focus was still very much on bonefish. When it comes to saltwater flats fishing, we Europeans were some way behind our American cousins.

My first opportunity came when fishing in the Seychelles in the early 2000s. Having sated my need to catch bonefish that day, my guide Serge Samson asked if I would like to try and catch a GT. I still remember the thrill I felt at his words, offering me the opportunity I had been waiting for. Up to this point, my flats experience had been limited to the major Caribbean fisheries, so

GT from the flats of Cosmoledo, Seychelles

when we headed away from the comparative safety of the shallows and began to wade deep in the surf line trying to spot GTs, I have to admit I was a little apprehensive. I was fully aware what other species were lurking in the spume and I had never before deep waded in the crashing white water. If someone told me then that 15 years later, every time I saw a shark I would run towards it instead of away from it, I would have thought they were quite mad!

Back then the hunting instinct kicked in, even though I really had no idea what I was looking for. Suddenly, out of nowhere, an electric blue shape against the green turtle grass appeared like an apparition in front of me. I was so shocked, my cast with the then very foreign 12# was not much more than a flop of 10ft and the fly landed in a dishevelled heap. Previous flats experience would dictate I had spooked my quarry with that cast, but this fish turned on it in a flash, engulfed the fly and took off to the surf line. The speed of the attack and the sheer power of that run completely took me by surprise as I hung on for dear life. I remember thinking at the time, 'This is incredible, I have to do this again!'

My first GT was not massive: a small 20lb fish – but it left me with such an overwhelming impression of the manner in which it was caught, and the power of that run, that I was hooked. Since then I have hunted GTs far and wide across the globe, from the Seychelles to Sudan to Christmas Island. Every trip I have done and every encounter I have had, I have strived to understand this extraordinary fish a little more. As a fly rod species, they are unique. Yes, tarpon get bigger and jump out of the water, sailfish and other billfish may run faster, but there is nothing that will prepare you for the speed with which GTs move on the flats. When they decide that they are going to eat, it's like a jet fighter kicking in an after-burner. The fish accelerates like a sprinter off the blocks, switching direction in a heartbeat. A quick flick of their long dorsal fins and then that big bucket mouth opens to engulf their prey. It is a sight that never gets old.

Tim Babich coined the phrase 'gangsters of the flats' which I feel is highly appropriate. They are the muggers that hide in dark corners, waiting to overcome unsuspecting prey as it passes by. They have a very unique character, and being an apex predator, are extremely opportunistic,

Wading along the edge on St Francois, Seychelles

centering on any prey source that is abundant in the location. They follow sharks, hunt on the backs of rays, corral baitfish in packs, eat everything from crabs to birds, and coming in off the ocean they can be truly fearless. Every time I have a close encounter, this incredible species has taught me something new.

Fishing for GTs, like any species you focus on, can become a bit of an obsession. The one thing I have learnt is that GT fishing is not an easy sport, and neither should it be. This fish is at the top of the food chain, and as such should be, in my opinion, fished for on that level. I suppose what I am trying to get across is that hunting this species on fly is not for everyone. A certain skill level is required and anglers should try and attain that base level before attempting to fish for them. I know this a slightly controversial view, but it is fairer on the fish and indirectly on the angler.

I feel it is also important to make the distinction between hunting GTs on the flats with a fly and hunting GTs in other environments. Many fishermen who encounter GTs on a day bluewater fishing, or hit them jigging or popping over structure, will tell you that there is not much to getting them to eat, and all you have to do is locate them to hook them. The only challenge then comes in actually landing them – so for this style of angling, they become an ideal target. In the same way, permit are equally easy to catch on a live crab, but as we well know, trying to persuade them to eat a fly can be soul-destroying. A GT is a totally different fish on the flats and has the potential to be far more cautious. They are not just the brutish eating machines that many make them out to be. In shallow water this species is far more challenging, and even though they have a distinctly aggressive nature, they can exhibit extraordinary cunning. Whether this comes from cognitive ability or just a self-preservation instinct in shallower water is difficult to ascertain, but do not underestimate their amazing ability to learn.

As a flyfishing tour operator and avid saltwater flats fisherman, I have been fortunate enough to fish with some of the pioneers of giant trevally fishing in the Pacific, Africa and Indian Ocean in numerous locations. Without their expert tutelage this book would not have been possible and I hope it will be a testament to their achievements. This tome is an attempt at recording

what these pioneers discovered, combined with some observations from my own time on the flats and the theories I have deduced from those experiences.

This book will introduce you to this outstanding species. It will describe their physical attributes, the environments they inhabit and hunt in, their prey species, some of their idiosyncrasies and habits and where to locate them. It will then move into an in-depth look at tackle and equipment, preparation, conservation and correct handling practices, different fishing strategies on the flats and in bluewater and then a focus on some of the other trevally species that can be targeted on fly. I will then show you some of the top destinations to go and hunt GTs. Although I have wonderful memories of many of these destinations myself, these chapters have been written by friends who were often instrumental in their discovery, operate them or spent a long time there. Some of their stories will captivate you.

Author's first GT

This information will aid you in tracking these magnificent fish down and will hopefully increase the odds of bumping into them yourself. You will then have the chance to develop your own theories. As with any type of fishing, no one has all the answers and every day is a school day. Once you have experienced the extraordinary take of one of these fish and the sheer power of their runs, it is hard not to fall in love with the trevally's pugnacious nature. If you have never hooked a GT on a fly, then you need to – it will change your life.

CHAPTER 2 - SPECIES DISTRIBUTION

Although closely related to Atlantic jack crevalle, giant trevally, along with many other trevally species, are found in the tropical and subtropical climates of the Indian Ocean and the Pacific. In the Indian Ocean you will find them from South Africa up the East African coastline into the Red Sea and Persian Gulf. From there they inhabit the Asian coastline of India, Sri Lanka, Pakistan, South East Asia and Indonesia and as far south as the northern coast of Australia. Most of the islands and pinnacles in the Indian Ocean from Mozambique, Seychelles and Madagascar across to the Andeman Islands support healthy populations.

Inshore rock and surf fishing dominates many of these areas, due to the rocky surf lines and deep water pinnacles. Although ideal for surf fishing, jigging and popping these areas often require the deep dredging or teasing method when flyfishing for giant trevally.

The next challenge is to find an area where subsistence fishing has not decimated the populations. Currently, the principal flats fisheries for giant trevally in the Indian Ocean are the Seychelles Islands, recently discovered Sudan and the outer islands of Mauritius. There are areas in the Maldives with huge potential, but fishing is not allowed on many of those islands, with the result that there are no dedicated fishing operations at this point, although a few are exploring. There are good populations in Oman and although it has mainly been fished conventionally, this too is evolving.

There are extensive populations of giant trevally in the central Indo-Pacific region, along with all the archipelagos and offshore islands including Indonesia, Philippines and Solomon Islands. Giant trevally are present in the oceans and reefs from Malaysia to Vietnam, but strangely not China. Their offshore range is seen as far north as Japan. Heading south, the species reaches as far as New South Wales in Australia and has been reported on the northern tip of New Zealand. GT distribution continues throughout the western Pacific, including Tonga, Western Samoa and Polynesia, with its western boundary limits known at this stage to be the Pitcairn and Hawaiian Islands. In early 2015, a giant trevally was caught off the coast of Panama in the eastern Pacific, suggesting that their geographic distribution could be broader than anticipated.

Surf-line of Cosmoledo, Seychelles

The flats of Christmas Island

White sand flats of Providence Atoll, Seychelles

For a long time, Christmas Island (Kiritimati) and Midway were the pioneering flyfisheries for GTs, but other atolls in the South Pacific have been explored as demand increases. Bikini Atoll, Kanton Atoll, Palmyra and a number of other obscure Pacific Islands have reported wonderful populations but are extremely difficult to get to. Islands in Tahiti and also Aitutaki in the Cook Islands have had flyfishermen cast their lines at GTs with some success, yet these fisheries are still in the developing stages. We eagerly await their coming of age as the need to find new and exciting destinations pushes the boundaries ever further. The Hawaiian Islands have long had a standing relationship with the GT where it is known as the Ulua; the species even being included in ancient rituals due to their warrior-like qualities. Unfortunately, their numbers have dwindled because of over-harvest.

The difficulty lies in trying to find a suitable environment to flyfish for them which is also accessible to fly anglers. Although possible to hunt along rocky shores and pinnacles, ideally we are looking for a flats environment to sight fish for giant trevally. We are constantly scouring for the next spot where this might be possible.

SPECIES DISTRIBUTION & DESTINATIONS

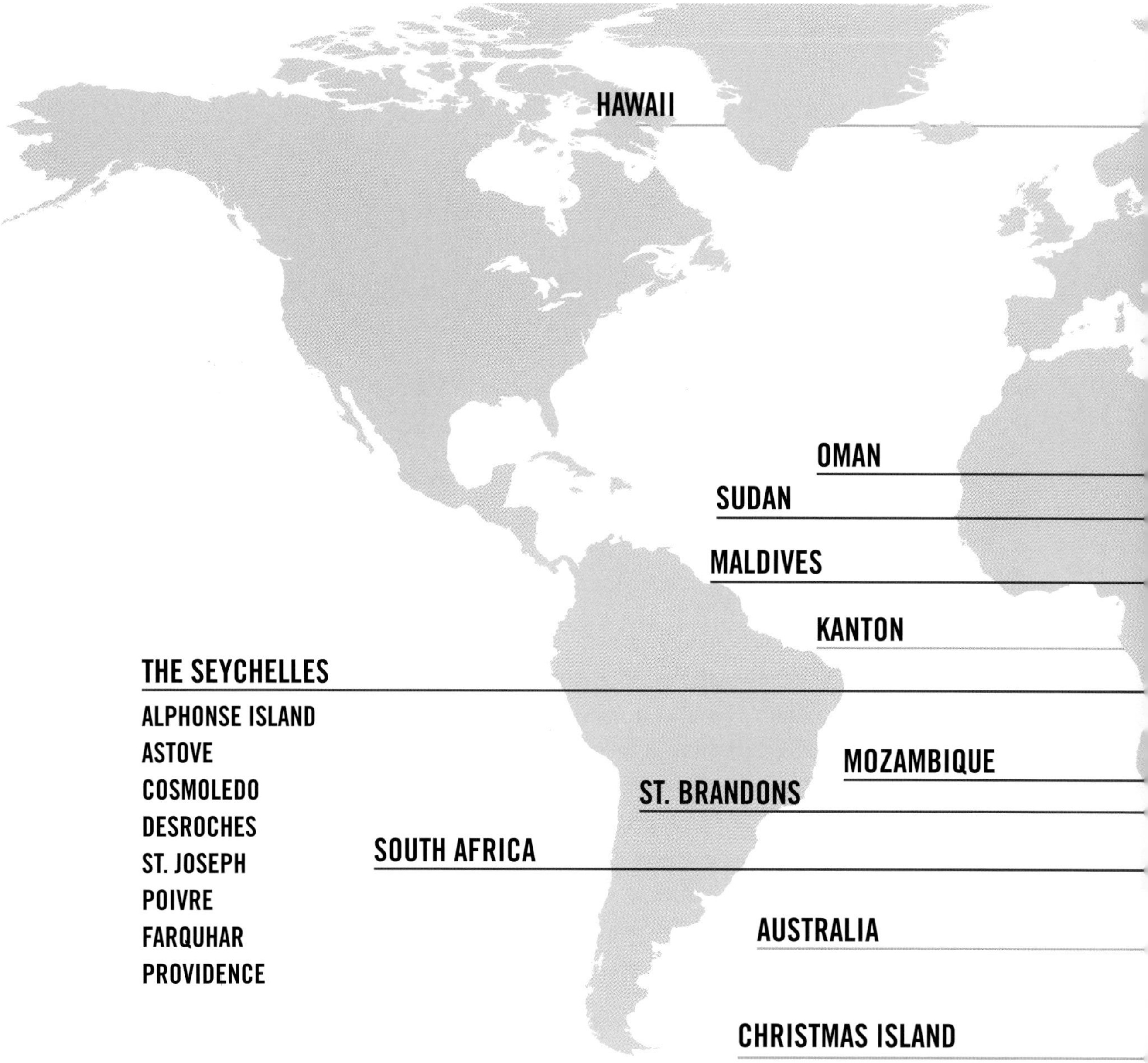

HAWAII

OMAN

SUDAN

MALDIVES

KANTON

THE SEYCHELLES

ALPHONSE ISLAND
ASTOVE
COSMOLEDO
DESROCHES
ST. JOSEPH
POIVRE
FARQUHAR
PROVIDENCE

MOZAMBIQUE

ST. BRANDONS

SOUTH AFRICA

AUSTRALIA

CHRISTMAS ISLAND

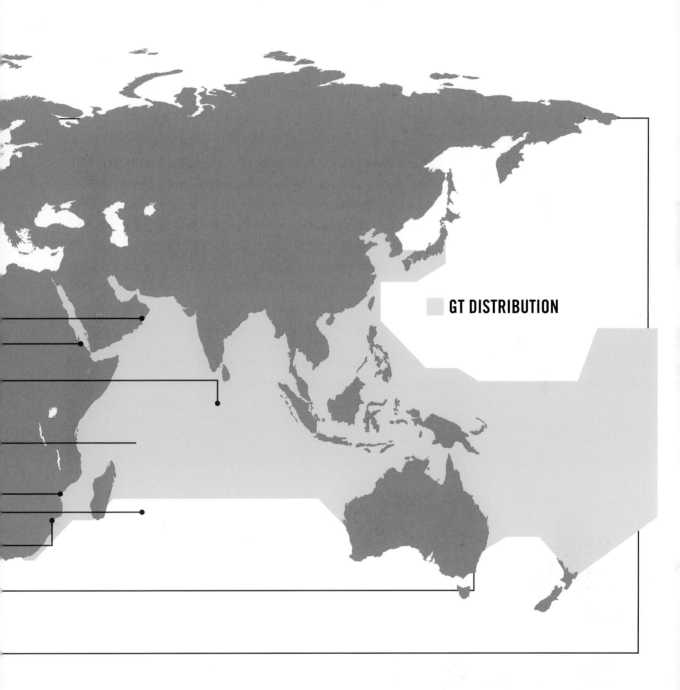

GT DISTRIBUTION

CHAPTER 3 - HISTORY OF GT FLYFISHING

Early records are hard to locate, but flyfishing for GTs most likely began in the Pacific Ocean on Christmas Island (Kiritimati). The earliest records there of fishermen actually targeting these predators on the fly is from the late 1970s. Fishermen flocked there as one of the first international flats destinations to open after the development of saltwater flyfishing in the Florida Keys and the Bahamas. I am sure that many people probably tried to catch trevally with traditional methods on the Hawaiian Islands where the species was revered before then, but very little has been documented. I can only imagine the experiences of those early flyfishing explorers, fresh from the Florida tarpon flats; happily bonefishing on some large expanse when out of left field a GT charged in and removed the prize from their line. The piscatorial version of a UFO sighting!

It was only a question of time before some of those flyfishermen tried specifically to target this mugger and they were completely astounded by their aggressive power. In the 1970s the first generation of guides operating out of the Captain Cook Hotel on the island began to unravel the GTs habits, patterns and even moods. Sometimes referred to as the 'Zen Masters of flyfishing' these early guides included such names as Simon Corrie, Big Eddie, Tebaki, Pilau, and of course Moana Kofe. Sadly some are no longer with us while others such as Simon and Moana are still

Michael Poor & Moana Kofe, Christmas Island

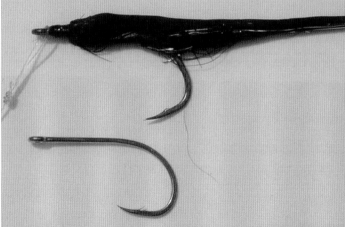

Early pioneer Tim Pask, Christmas Island

guiding. These pioneers of the sport were the first to begin to think about how to specifically target GTs and unlock their mystery. A handful of their clients became equally obsessed and began to dedicate some serious time and effort to landing these beasts.

At that time the tackle used was adapted from the tarpon flats, so 10-12# rods, saltwater lines of the time which required regular application of silicone to make them shoot in the tropical heat; light braided cores and light shock tippet with IGFA class tippets would have been the order of the day. To land a GT on this light gear, especially light flyline cores, meant many cut or snapped lines. It must have been exceptionally tough, making the achievements only more laudable. Up to this point, GT fishing was conducted for an evening giggle at 'cocktail time'. The original 'local special' was a piece of white PVC piping threaded with 80lb wire and a massive treble hook. Local guides would hold clients up in the surf to prevent them being knocked down and lacerated on the sharp coral.

Early fly patterns were also adapted from tarpon fishing, yellow and red deceivers and cockroach patterns being favoured. Smaller hook sizes such as 1/0 and 2/0 were preferred for their greater penetration as there were none of the cutting point hooks we have today. A small band of dedicated anglers appeared such as Richard Humphrey, Jerry Swanson, Lance and Randall Kaufmann, Tim Pask and a few others who spent nearly all their time hunting these fish above all other species. Richard Humphrey would target GTs for two weeks a year, twice a year, and held the IGFA record for a time of 62lb landed on a 10# as his guide was carrying his 12# at the time! They believed that if you wanted to hunt for them specifically then rather than have the guide carry the 12# and carry an 8# then you needed to have the 12# in your hand all the time or when the opportunity arose it would be missed. These dedicated few, along with a handful of converts, began to explore some of the other Pacific fisheries such as Midway Island, Bikini Atoll and Kanton Island. Although Midway's primary focus was marlin and the bluewater fishery, Captain Ed Hughes and some intrepid anglers explored the eight-kilometre-square lagoon and hit some massive GTs in the mid 1990s.

From the mid 1980s, GTs were also being fished for in South Africa and other countries along the Eastern African cast line. Referred to as iggies, ignoblis, kingies or kingfish, fishing for them was concentrated in the reef surf line and estuaries, a tricky environment at the best of times. As there are no areas of typical flats, it made hunting particularly tough, with GTs being considered a huge prize. One of the very first of these dedicated anglers was Andy Coetzee who has since gone on to be a household name in GT flyfishing in South Africa. He was part of an elite group of 'Kingie catchers' headed up by Lance Rorick, who caught the first GT over 10kg on fly on a 9# in the Kosi lakes in late 1985. The movement gathered momentum with men like the late Keith Miller, Richard Schumann and Jake Alletson, all of whom had an influence on which patterns to tie for these voracious predators.

Andy Coetzee in the South African surf

As Andy was living and working down in Kosi, he was able to dedicate a huge amount of time on the water and in the surf, experimenting with fly sizes, colours and styles. To begin with, inspiration came from Lefty Kreh's book *Flyfishing in Saltwater* and they copied his deceiver patterns along with full-sized poppers. Very quickly these were modified and Andy developed flies called Kosi chartreuse deceivers, Hardy head deceivers, Epoxy sprats and poppers. The biggest sizes were 1/0 to 2/0 in the early years of 1985. He began fishing with a very mismatched #9 weight rod matched with a tiny Okuma fly reel and floating line. Needless to say in the surf environment this outfit did not last long. He then coined the phrase 'go big or go home' and started on a composite development 10# rod from NZ with a Martin reel. That lasted a few months until he upgraded to a G Loomis 12# with a Lamson #3 reel and intermediate Airflo line with fly sizes jumping up to 3/0 and 4/0 34700 Mustad hooks. He beefed up from 20lb tippet (which proved to be just wasting time) to 45lb maxima.

Poppers were very popular, although Andy felt shank-tied poppers were too cumbersome to cast and when the kingies smashed into the popper they invariably 'blew' the popper away with the splash of water trying to engulf it. He began to use popping heads, a bullet-shaped popper slid up the line so it could be used as a 'chugger type' or 'slider' head, depending on the wind conditions. Different size popping heads could be changed to suit the conditions. They also developed the African-style stripping basket comprised of a big washing basket deep enough to stop the line from blowing out, combined with thick nylon spikes glued to the bottom to stop it tangling. The critical thing for these early surf flyfishermen was putting the fly into the productive zone which Andy and others learned through trial and error. Timing the cast was the critical aspect, as casting into rolling breakers achieved nothing but tangled lines. It was imperative to false cast until the wave passed then to drop the fly into the white churned-up, productive water.

The early African pioneers had their work cut out as the reefs were close and as soon as they hooked a fish, it would charge off to the reef edge and cut the line. Andy became tired of losing flies and decided to try not giving any line and hold on for dear life, straight sticking the fish and using the power from the butt of the rod. Thus, some might say, the modern method of fighting GTs on a flyrod was born. In the early years of the mid-1980s there were no more than a handful flyfishing the salt. Jake Alletson, Richard Schumann, Andrew Parsons, Mark Yelland, Joni Botha, MC Coetzer and the late Keith Miller were some of the pioneer saltwater and trevally flyfishermen who have since gone down in South African fishing folklore. GTs became *the* fish to catch on a fly and they have continued to be revered in South Africa ever since.

Exploring anglers moved their way up the coast-line and the archipelagos of Bazaruto and Benguerra in Mozambique became popular. It was in early 1986 that Sabal Lodge opened in Mozambique and a few guides earned great reputations from guiding there. Although not classic flyfishing, such skilled practitioners as Andrew Parsons, Guy Ferguson, Anthony Diplock and MC Coetzee developed the technique of dredging with fast-sinking lines and heavy rods. Andrew started guiding on Bazaruto in 1995. GTs were his target, but he had a lot to learn. From his surf fishing days he knew they loved fast-moving surface lures so he fished mostly poppers to begin with. As there were very few giant poppers available then, he had some conversations with Murray Pedder, one of the foremost fly tiers at the time. He started using what was known as a 'Master Blaster' made in kit form by Edgewater Poppers. It was essentially a billfish popper but Andrew used it for some time very successfully for GTs, catching a good number around the one metre length mark.

Deep fishing, or dredging as it is now known, came about from Andrew's scuba diving. It became obvious to him that all the big fish around the Bazaruto and Benguerra archipelago were deep. The only time they caught them higher up would be when these big bruisers were pushing bait to the surface. He started working on getting his lines deep and made bigger and heavier flies. The technique proved extremely effective in hunting GTs off rock pinnacles and structures in deep water otherwise inaccessible to fly anglers.

Iconic Tam Tam catamaran

It was not until the early-to-mid 1990s that the Indian Ocean fisheries came into play. Early exploration was done entirely by live-aboard charter vessels as there were no structures on most of the atolls. The first pioneers heading in that direction found huge quantities of completely naive GTs on virgin flats which pretty much ate anything thrown at them. They must have thought they had died and gone to heaven and there are many of us who would have given just about anything to be part of the early exploration of these places. Some of those pioneers of the Pacific such as Jerry Swanson and Brian O'Keefe ventured out to these atolls, along with Jon Fisher from Urban Angler in New York. In the late 1990s, Martin Lewis built the catamaran *Tam Tam* which they used as a live-aboard charter to Alphonse Island, and they began to explore this phenomenal fishery.

In 1996 Larry Dahlberg went to the Seychelles to film his *The Hunt for Big Fish* TV programme. In addition to Martin and Anna Lewis and *Tam Tam*, the yacht *High Aspect* with Capt. Keith Jones was part of support of this expedition, as they had a desalination plant on board along with charging capacity needed for filming this show. What blew every one away and made them say 'sign me up for that!' was Larry Dahlberg, saying 'This bonefish is fighting twice as hard as the last one', and then reached for the leader which had two flies and two fish on one cast! That first Seychelles trip sold out 10 days after the Kaufmann's catalogue came out. It was the spring of 1998; anglers were Richard Humphrey, Brian O'Keefe, Jerry Swanson and others. GTs, bluefin trevally, numerous bonefish up to 10lb and about 20 species total were caught on that trip. There were no guides or guidebooks and numerous charters followed on the *High Aspect* fishing St Francois lagoon.

In 2000 an exploratory trip aboard the *High Aspect* to Farquhar, Cosmoledo and a couple of other atolls followed. Fishing was of course crazy good. Again no guides on this trip. There were fish that had never seen a fly or a person. GTs and bonefish would compete for the same 1/0 fly! Schools of smaller GTs (15-20lb) would come on the flats with the incoming tide and hunt like a pack of wolves. The Trey Combs Sea Habit Bucktail and variations on it were key flies at that time. In addition, when the fish were in the right mood, fishing poppers for GTs was as good as it gets.

In 1997 Tim Pilcher and well-known author Trey Combs along with anglers such as Steve Abel mounted live-aboard expeditions to the French-owned Clipperton Atoll approximately 1,000 miles due south of Cabos San Lucas. Three nights sailing had them fishing one of the most prolific sport fisheries on the planet. Although their main target was yellow fin tuna on the fly, there were significant bluefin trevally caught on these expeditions. On one of these trips in early 2000, a young Keith Rose-Innes gained a love for long distance live-aboard trips. One of the most important aspects that came from these Clipperton trips was the development of tackle and equipment. Trey Combs and Steve Abel perfected rigging heavy duty fly gear to tackle tuna and gave much of the inspiration to Trey's book *Bluewater Flyfishing* which remains to this day the authoritative tome on big fish on fly gear. It taught so many of us about rigging, much of which has later been adapted to GT fishing.

The remote Clipperton Atoll, Pacific

Keith Rose-innes
Arno Mathee
Gerhard Laubscher

In 2000 the Alphonse Island resort was opened which at last put a fully-fledged guide team on one of these atolls over a five month season. Suddenly a number of exceptional guides were thrown together for an extended period of time with a lot of fish and anglers to experiment on. The result was a rapid jump forward in learning, experience and the opportunity for experimentation. Arno Mathee, Wayne Haselau and Serge Sampson were amongst some of the very first guides on Alphonse. Since then many great names in GT guiding have come off that atoll. In 2005 Keith Rose-Innes began to explore the outer Island on the Yacht *Meike* where I bumped into him as he stopped by on Alphonse where I was hosting a group. Keith and I had become acquainted in Farlows and Russia a few years before.

Keith, along with his partners Arno Mathee and Gerhard Laubscher, went on to build the first fully-fledged operations targeting GTs specifically in the Seychelles. Firstly they explored Farquhar, and then the outer atolls of Cosmoledo and Providence. It was a golden age in the Indian Ocean with unheard-of numbers of GTs being caught on the fly. Astove Atoll was then added to the list as part of the Cosmoledo experience. Just after Cosmoledo came online on the ill-fated *Indian Ocean Explorer* I took my first groups and the experience was mind-numbing. Not long after my last visit to the outer atolls in 2008, the Indian Ocean began to experience issues with piracy from Somalia and all live-aboard vessels were shut down. This pulled the focus back onto Farquhar Atoll in the Seychelles and led Arno Mathee and Gerhard Laubscher to began to look elsewhere. They discovered the extraordinary atoll of St Brandon's in Mauritius. Although the prime focus was on the big bonefish there, it still has a reputation for massive GTs.

In December 2003 an exploratory trip out to the Coral Sea in Australia was conducted by Damon Olsen from Nomad Sportfishing. Although Damon and his team had been operating since 2000, they had mostly focused on popping and jigging for GTs, but after this initial trip, Damon built the 80ft Mothership *Odyssey* to continue exploring this area in 2005 and reports began to flood in of monster trevally being caught around the rock pinnacles and structure there. Although most of these fish were too large to be landed on fly, there are many who tried and some have been successful, with truly extraordinary results.

Throughout this period, major developments were made in tackle, flylines and reel drags, all contributing factors to making the difficult task of landing these bruisers slightly easier. The flyfishing community embraced trevally as a prime target and now feelers began to push out in many directions.

New areas are being discovered as potential GT hotspots all the time, although perhaps in some case the infrastructure is not quite there yet. The Middle East has shown a lot of promise, with Oman and especially the Nubian Flats of Sudan showing healthy populations and huge flats to hunt them on. Keith Clover and Rob Scott alongside the incomparable Nicola Vitali and Federico Castignoli planned their exploratory trips to Sudan in 2012, although the Italians had already been exploring the area for conventional fishing for a considerable time. Later they also explored the island of Secotra in Yemen before the conflict shut it down, reporting massive GTs. The Sudan is perhaps the latest destination to hit the market and it is exciting to see how it develops.

The end of the piracy threat in the Somali basin has allowed the Seychelles atolls only reached by live-aboard to now become home to land-based operations such as the lodge on Astove Atoll and the planned building on Cosmoledo. I think the next major discoveries will come from the Pacific as many of those atolls once thought of as inaccessible have suddenly become easier to get to and more economically viable, such as Aitiutaki and Kanton. It will be fascinating to see how the pursuit of these incredible fish drives us to yet more remote areas of the globe in our search. I can't wait!

Indian Ocean Explorer on Assumption Atoll, Seychelles

CHAPTER 4 - THE BIOLOGY OF GTs

As their name indicates, GTs can grow to huge proportions and are a near-perfect predator. GTs have a laterally (side-to-side) compressed body, suggesting that they are both good at burst swimming and agile turns. The fact that their pectoral fins can tuck against their bodies to lower their profile hints at this as well. The large bucket mouth contains well-placed piercing teeth giving way to a broad domed forehead with large all-seeing eyes. The upper jaw has a series of strong outer canines with an inner band of smaller teeth. The lower jaw contains a single row of conical teeth, the perfect weaponry for a slashing strike. The eyes of the giant trevally have a horizontal streak in which ganglion and photoreceptor cell densities are in far greater numbers than the rest of the eye. It is believed this allows the fish to gain a panoramic view of its surroundings, removing the need to constantly move the eye. This facilitates detection of prey or predators in their field of view.

The dorsal fin is split into two parts and the powerful heavy-set oval body tapers rapidly to a thick caudal peduncle (some anglers call this the wrist) covered in sharp scutes. The curved tail has the ability to propel it through the water at extraordinary speeds. These characteristics make GTs the ideal predator on the flats, the only thing above them being sharks and Man. Although GTs are sprinters, they also possess extraordinary endurance and agility, and will never give in. These thugs can be found hunting in packs, chasing down their quarry in bursts of speed and competing against each other to hit their prey. I have even seen them try to take a fly out of the

mouth of a fish already hooked. They are an exceptionally hardy species and have been known to smash into hard coral in the surf and also to beach themselves to smash their prey. These encounters often leave battle scars around their heads.

The giant trevally is the largest member of the genus Caranx, similar in shape to a number of other large jacks and trevallys and the fifth-largest member of the family Carangidae. It is not uncommon to tangle with fish as large as 150lb in weight and specimens over 200lb with a fork length of 170cm have been recorded. Specimens this size are very rare, with the species only occasionally seen at lengths over a metre and highly prized. Only three individuals over 100lb have been reported to the IGFA, but many more have been landed and released in the Indian Ocean and Pacific.

You will notice that GTs have different colours, predominantly either a bluish-grey colour to that of dark black. There is much speculation as to why this is, although the original theory was that the black fish are males and the blue-grey fish are females. When smaller than 50cm it is said the giant trevally is a silvery-grey fish, with the head and upper body slightly darker in both sexes. When they grow over 50cm it is believed they show sexual dimorphism in their colouration. Males exhibit dusky to jet-black bodies, while females are a much lighter-coloured silvery-grey. Individuals with darker dorsal colouration often also display striking silvery striations and markings on the upper part of their bodies, particularly their backs. Black dots of a few millimetres in diameter may be found scattered all over the body, although the coverage of these dots varies between widespread to none at all. All the fins are generally light grey to black, although I have noticed fish with bright white dorsal fins. This I put down to older fish that have spent a lot of time hunting on the flats until they have actually sun-bleached their dorsal fins.

Aggressive posturing

However, it may also be that GTs will change colour when in different environments and also perhaps with moods. This may also be the source of the colour variation described previously (not sexual dimorphism). Infrequently will you find black GTs caught on the flats or shown in photographs. Often you will find images of fish that are blue-grey with black speckles. My own theory is that GTs change colour, like bonefish, to adapt to the colour scheme of the environment that they hunt in, hence the speckled effect. I have for a while believed that their colour is mood related. Alternatively the different markings may literally just be individual. GTs hugging the backs of rays are often black, and another opinion is that these fish are actively aggressive and will take a fly. It has been observed that if you hook these dark fish sometimes they have reverted to a grey colour by the time they are landed. Guides have seen GTs swim onto the flats silver, find a ray and turn black as soon as they take up station. When swimming together in schools such as the Farquhar pets it may also be that the males turn black to the show their dominance or show off to the females, a little like a mating display. As males do not often grow as large as females it may make them appear larger, a little like a bird shaking out its plumage. James Christmas witnessed a particular fish amongst these pets displaying its dominance by flashing from silver to black four times while at the same time raising its dorsal fin. Even though it was not the largest fish, the other backed off and left it alone. He has also seen GTs 'gape' with their mouths open, much like a trout, to show dominance to other individuals.

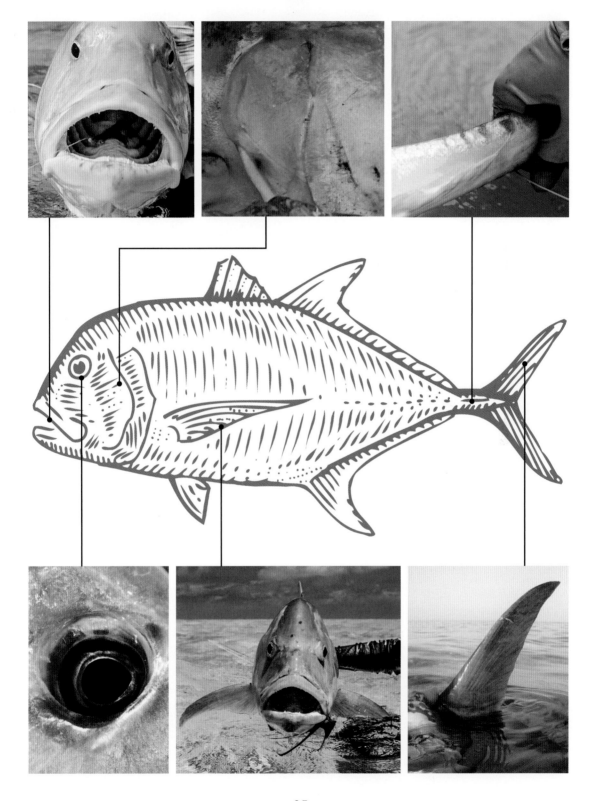

CHAPTER 5 - WHAT DO TREVALLY EAT?

When it comes to prey species, there is very little that this swimming garbage-can-of-a-fish won't eat. They are extremely opportunistic and will zero in on any local food source. They also seem to have an ability to remember when that food source is cyclical in nature. There have been a number of scientific papers written on the subject of percentage stomach contents of different fish species, Cephalopoda and Crustacea – but really the only need from a flyfisherman's perspective is to know what they eat so that we can imitate it effectively.

In this regard, GTs help us out significantly because, unlike trout which can become fixated on certain phases of insect hatches, the omnivorous and opportunistic nature of a trevally removes the need for this fine detail. If they are hungry and are presented with a food offering, generally they will eat it. The percentages of fish to crustaceans, Cephalopoda to molluscs and a category we shall just call 'others' really depends in which ocean they swim and the availability of that particular food. For example scientific studies have stated that trevally in the Pacific islands such as around Hawaii, Christmas Island, Palamyra and others have a higher percentage of crustaceans in their diets than, for example, those living in the Indian Ocean which have a higher percentage of fish species.

All trevally will eat small fish, from parrotfish and wrasse species along the reef-edge to hunting mullet and bonefish on the flats. Numerous bonefishermen have had their prize catch swallowed whole by a charging GT and been left dazed and confused. Mullet are amongst their favourite fish species though, so if you can find backwaters where these fish congregate, then at some point GTs will show up. Juvenile milkfish are also a favourite, especially on Christmas Island, along with a huge number of snapper species. In areas of Hawaii certain species of fusiliers are also a particular favourite. But in the absence of these favourites, GTs will eat pretty much any species that cross their path. Stomach contents from research in Hawaii and Australia have proved as much.

GT snacks, school of mullet

On the GT menu, clockwise from top left: Baby turtles, Crab sticks, puffed Puffer fish, Mantis shrimp, Bonefish, Hermit crab, Coral species, Sooty terns

After fish, crustaceans make up a large proportion of a trevally's diet. There are numerous crabs such as blue crabs and swimming crabs that they will zone in on. They will also forage out mantis shrimp, glass and grass shrimp amongst turtle grass, and prawns on the flats bed. Divers have witnessed larger specimens tackle lobster in the defensive position without worrying too much.

Cephalapods such as octopus, squid and cuttlefish around the reef edges are a valued food item, but trevally will also snaffle bivalve molluscs such as snails that make their home on the reef. In certain areas of Australia and New Zealand, their stomach contents have even revealed large quantities of echinoderms or urchins!

'Others' really is slightly telling as some studies have revealed spiders and insects having featured on the menu and they have been witnessed to target birds. On Farquhar Atoll in the Seychelles

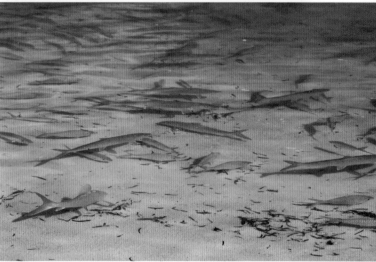

the GTs have learned about the nesting cycle of the sooty tern. There is a huge population of sooty terns that nest on Goulette Island. On numerous occasions, big fish have been witnessed coming in on the waves from the ocean, hanging around until they target a fledgling or even a fully-grown specimen, tracking it and then taking it from the air in one hit before returning to the ocean to digest the meal. It has been witnessed too frequently to be a one-off phenomenon.

On another occasion, on Assumption Atoll a fisherman was wandering along the beach peering into the surf when behind him he heard a rustling. Out from below the sand appeared a tiny turtle … followed by another … and another. The beach was soon covered in little turtles all making their way to the surf line. As soon as they hit the water, the first GTs showed up. They savaged every baby turtle that made it to the sea while he was there, and he caught eight fish in the feeding frenzy that ensued.

CHAPTER 6 - TACKLE AND EQUIPMENT

So what kind of gear is necessary to stand up to these creatures of piscatorial nightmares? The best... When it comes to GT fishing if there is any defect in your gear, it will be discovered in the first ten seconds of the fight. I have witnessed some catastrophic tackle failures over many different brands. On Astove I saw a rod 'go' in the tip section, and then shatter into six pieces down the blank with the angler landing the fish on a reel and one foot of rod. On Farquhar I saw a top brand reel quite literally smoke as the cork plate disintegrated, leaving metal on metal shrieking like a banshee. When you finally hook into a GT, the pressure that it applies to your equipment almost immediately is unlike any other fishing experience. So much effort has been taken to get you to this point that it is extremely frustrating to lose a fish because of tackle failure, especially as it is often your pride and joy that you have spent the previous six months selecting. My advice is: do not scrimp on your gear. You have travelled a very long way to catch these fish. Make sure you have the best gear you can afford.

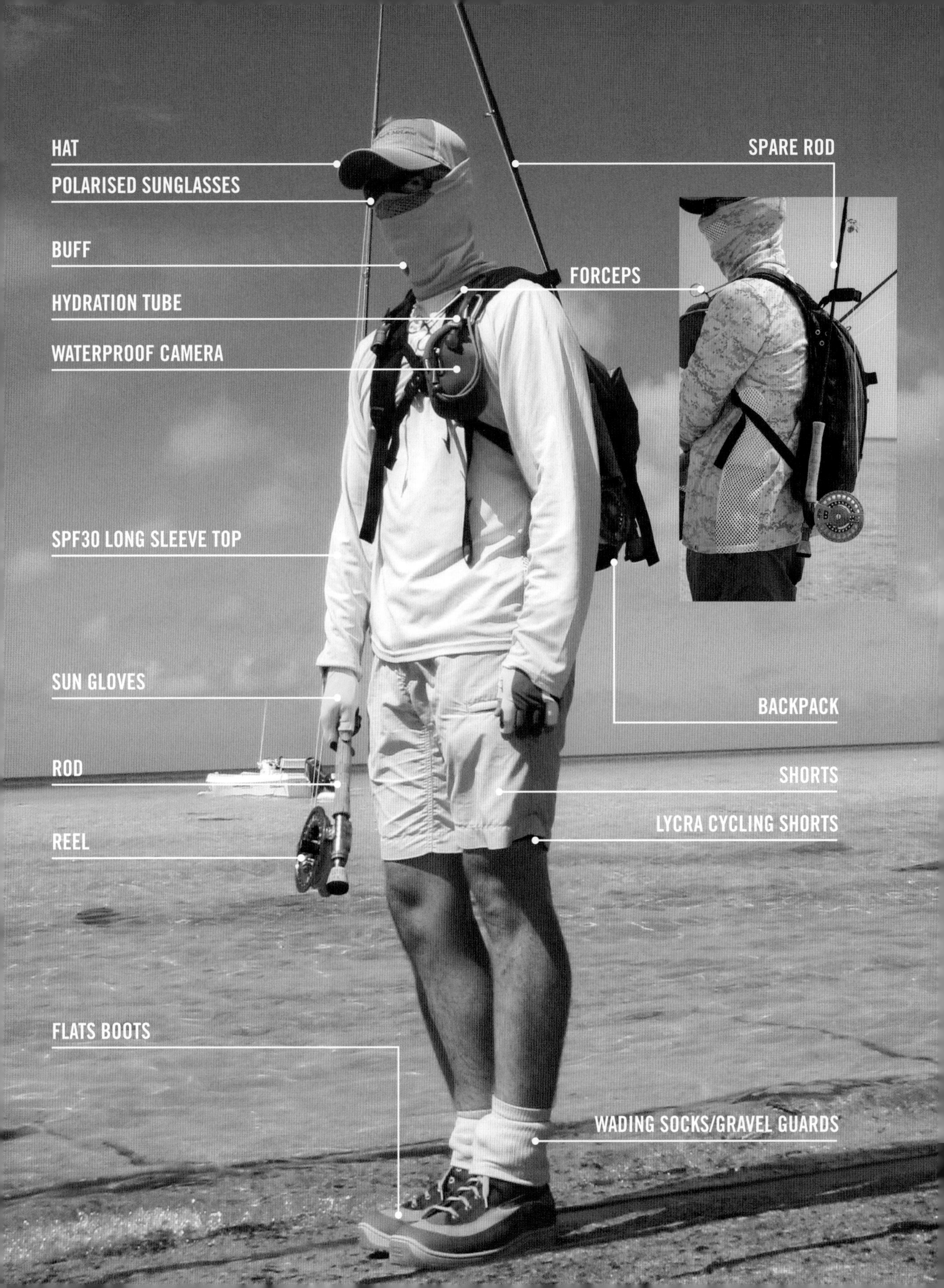

HAT

POLARISED SUNGLASSES

BUFF

HYDRATION TUBE

WATERPROOF CAMERA

SPF30 LONG SLEEVE TOP

SUN GLOVES

ROD

REEL

FLATS BOOTS

SPARE ROD

FORCEPS

BACKPACK

SHORTS

LYCRA CYCLING SHORTS

WADING SOCKS/GRAVEL GUARDS

RODS

The standard rod for GT fishing is 9' four piece 12#. If you are in the enviable position to be able to use a one piece rod then so much the better, but for most of us travelling on aircraft to reach GT habitat, it is not practical. For a long time I preferred a rod with a fore grip so that I could relax my arm during the battle. However over the last couple of years I have taken a leaf out of the Florida Keys tarpon fishermen's book. I came to realise that by using a fore grip I was reducing the length of the blank I could actually use. By holding the normal grip and placing the rod further down my hip I found I could apply even more pressure along the whole blank. Unlike many forms of flyfishing where the rod is really a deliverance tool for the fly and a mild shock absorber, when fishing for GTs it is necessary to use a rod that can really apply pressure to the fish. The more pressure that can be applied, the shorter the fight, the fresher the fish is when released. You will be amazed as to the amount of pressure that you can actually apply, but the angles are key.

Wade GT reel

The lower the plane of the rod, the more pounds pressure can be brought to bear on the fish. I think the first time I really thought about this was when Andy Mill demonstrated it effectively in his series *Chasing Silver*. He hooked his 12# up to a bucket and pulley and by changing the angles could exert maximum pressure in a battle.

When I began flyfishing, flyrod technology was nothing like as advanced as it has now become. The rods we all aspired to own were the Sage graphite or Loomis GL3s. They were considered the fastest actions available, and they were head and shoulders above the competition. I know this somewhat dates me, but I think I started flyfishing just as technology had done the big jump to carbon fibre from fibre glass, and rods were not only exciting but also in a state of flux.

Over the last 20 years the science behind our art has leapt forward exponentially. Line classes, weight and more importantly, strength, have come a long way. The advent of new resin technology such as nano titanium, means that much stronger rods can be produced than ever before. They also happen to be very light. For larger line classes this is an amazing breakthrough as we can now have a rod capable of dealing with larger fish but which still handles like a flyrod and not a

poker. What I find intriguing is that many fishermen have not moved with it. I am also a real fan of rods with Titanium Recoil rings. Not only are they light, but the fact they bend when pulling heavy tippet materials and knots through them is a huge bonus and has helped me land fish I would have otherwise lost.

The 12# is still the standard rod to go, as it has enough backbone to deal with most situations. On the flats I have now switched to an 11#. It has proved to have more than enough power in the butt section to deal with a big GT. Casting all day with a 12# can be very hard work. Unlike a 12# it is still a casting tool rather than just a fish-wrestler and is even capable of light presentations if the need arises.

In the surf line, drop-offs, or areas easily accessible to the ocean where very large specimens may appear, it is still recommended to take a 12# as in these situations you are going to have to apply far more pressure to prevent being shredded through the coral and cut off. When fishing offshore rock pinnacles and structure, it is also advisable to stick to a 12# or even a 14# for extra lifting power over the gunwales of a boat.

There are many great brands of flyrod on the market at the time of writing, but my favoured rods of choice would be Sage Xi3 or the new Salt, Loop cross, Loomis Crosscurrent GLX or NRX. My personal favourite is the Hardy Proaxis series for which I was a consultant through its testing phase, and the new Hardy Zephrus which are more refined. Not only are they extremely light and nicely finished (we all love our toys…) but are exceptionally strong and very rarely break.

Hardy SDS 12000

REELS

When it comes to a reel for GT fishing, again, make it the best you can afford. The reel is perhaps the most important piece of kit you are investing in as, without a low start-up inertia and very powerful drag, this is going to be the factor that determines success or failure. You can land a fish on a smashed rod, but if your reel goes, you are toast. In some situations it is necessary to actually lock up the reel and fight the fish to a standstill.

When I look at a 12# reel there are several key elements I focus on. With so many reels on the market these days it can be a minefield. Firstly I want a reel that can take being bashed around in the surf, dropped in the sand and still perform without jamming. Although in the early days a large cork calliper disc drag pressed against the reel spool was the way forward, I have since seen cork disintegrate with extended use, and also compress, reducing the effectiveness of the drag. When Trey Combs was writing *Bluewater Flyfishing* in the 1990s, cork calliper drags were seen as revolutionary, as they were adapted from big game fishing. At the time these drag systems produced low start-up inertia and a smooth drag unlike anything present at the time. Over the last five years, carbon fibre plates have begun to replace cork which always made perfect sense to me. What material do we use in car brakes? Carbon fibre is hard-wearing, relatively heat-resistant and does not deteriorate over time. Although I like simple drag mechanisms, I also recognise that at the time of writing many modern drags are completed sealed. This means that inside that sealed drag will be numerous carbon fibre plates which, simply by the laws of physics, create a larger surface area and therefore can exert more pressure.

Unlike tarpon fishing where class tippets are involved, we are normally using very heavy mono leaders. The ability to adjust the drag with finesse during a battle is not necessary. Tarpon fishermen require the ability to set their drag to a specific pound breaking strain to match their class tippets. Delicate adjustment to a maximum of 16lb is all they require. I want a drag in my reels that can go from start to lock-up with one turn on the drag knob. There are times I have had the drag cranked as far as I could and I am not capable of physically pulling line off the reel but a GT has screamed line off as if it was nothing. No room for class tippets here, unless you like disappointment.

Next I look at how the spool is attached to spindle and the cage. A pop fitting or small catch is simply not going to cut it, and too many times have I seen the spool fly off, to the horror of an angler, spewing line as it goes. I like a reel where there is one single spindle that screws down or some sort of solid screw mechanism that means that spool is going nowhere. I also favour a large arbour reel which is going to give a fast speed of retrieve on each revolution of the handle. I personally also prefer direct drive reels over multipliers – less to go wrong and normally lighter. It should be capable of holding at least 350 yards of 50lb Dacron or 80lb braid – *at least*. There are times you need every yard.

At the time of writing, preferred reels would be Hardy Fortuna, Charlton Mako, Abel super 12, Tibor Gulfstream quick change, Shilton SL7, Wade GT and Hardy SDS. All of these I have seen very few failures on, if any, and they will get the job done. There are other top class manufacturers but not all reels will withstand spending days on end fully submerged.

Charlton Mako

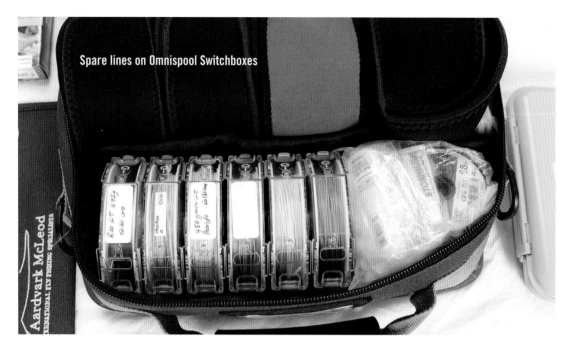

Spare lines on Omnispool Switchboxes

FLYLINES

It is very rarely necessary to use anything other than a floating line when fishing for GTs, unless you are dredging. Some fishermen discuss the merits of clear intermediates or ghost tips, but in reality they can be a hindrance rather than a blessing. We are not standing on the front of a skiff here, where we can stack the line in a foot-well sheltered from the wind. We are normally up to our waist in water in the surf line. Not only would anything other than a floating line sink while we wade, and immediately wrap itself around anything it can find, but if you are putting that cast out to a fast-moving target and for some reason the shot does not go according to plan, you then have to strip all that line back in, and roll it up onto the surface before being able to recast. Too late, you have missed your chance.

When GTs first came into the cross hairs, normal tarpon equipment was called into service and this included flylines. Most flylines are built on either a 30lb braid or mono core. Recently it has become obvious that this is not strong enough, as GTs can take off at such speed that the angler is unprepared and lines have parted. The fish will also always do its best to wrap you around the nearest obstacle it can find, so a need for a heavier core was quickly recognised and specialised lines have since appeared built on 50lb cores to aid with abrasion resistance during the battle.

The Airflo GT line has provided excellent service, and more recently I designed a line for RIO, the RIO GT. I am not a fan of short head lengths and bullet tapers. Although these heavier tapers turn over large flies more easily, they tend to have short heads and thin running line which can be irritating in the surf. The thin running line becomes twisted, and as it is a short taper designed to be shot off the front of a skiff, once the cast is made, all the running line needs to be stripped back before the line can be recast. I therefore designed a taper more along the lines of a long bellied distance line that could be picked back quickly off the surface and recast, while still capable of turning over a heavy fly. So the RIO GT was born. Flylines are a personal choice as to what works for the angler and their particular set-up. For me, I have found the 400 grain RIO GT works beautifully with a 10 or 11#, the 475 grain on the 12# and the 550 grain on 14# or more.

For dredging you need the fastest sinking line you can find to get down in the water column. For this style of fishing you are looking for a 600-700 grain line that will get down fast in a current. I have not found a better one than the Airflo depth-finder series which are made on a big game 70lb core. As you often find yourself attached to mother earth with this style of fishing, the stronger core the better.

RIGGING A GT SET-UP

When setting a line up for GT fishing, you need to be aware that it is going to get abused, and quite possibly cut on coral. Therefore it is imperative it can be changed quickly on the flats while in the water. For backing in the past I used 50lb Dacron for a little extra security on abrasion. It takes up quite a lot of space on the spool though, so you are looking at more like 250 yards on a 12-weight reel rather than 350 yards. I have had occasions where I was distinctly nervous I would be spooled.

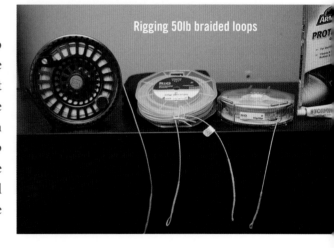

Rigging 50lb braided loops

Then gelspun backing transferred from bluewater fishing and many people began to switch to it. The problem with gelspun, apart from the cost, is that it is too thin. If you get a loop of that wrapped around your thumb with a charging fish, it is likely to cut you right to the bone. The other issue I have is that unless the loops are very carefully tripled up, it will cut into the flyline. I saw a client once who had rigged his own gear and had tripled up when he made his loop. Once the fish was on the backing, the single strand braid loop sliced straight through the braided loop on the end of his line and he lost the fish – and the line.

These days I have switched to using 80lb spinning braid such as Tufline or Powerpro. The 80lb is not too thin, but I can still get 650 yards on a 12-weight reel. I had an instance on Depose

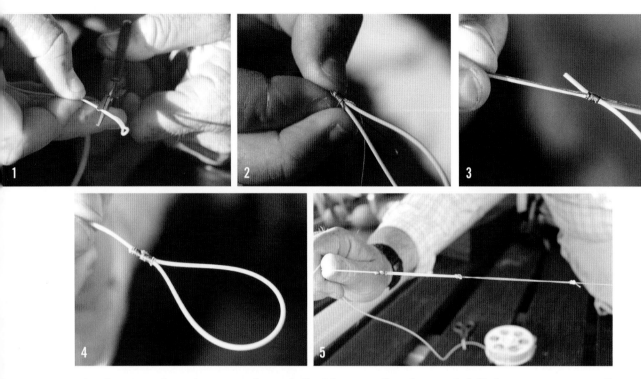

Island on Farquhar where I nearly used all of that as well and it nearly killed me retrieving it. All backing should be put on tight with an automatic line winder. If you try and spool it by hand, not only is it extremely hard work, but if it is not on tight enough it can cut into itself in the middle of battle and lock up, ending the battle sharpish. Most people don't own an electric line winder, so I recommend taking it to your nearest tackle shop and have them do it.

As it is quite often necessary to change a line on the flats, so loop-to-loop connections make everything simple. I therefore use a doubled-up bimini twist on the end of the backing with a loop large enough to put the entire reel through and a loop-to-loop connection on the end of the flyline. That way if you need to change a line it is very simple and fast.

Some lines come with welded loops on them. I am afraid I still don't trust them as I saw too many fail in the early days and they are not large enough for large diameter leader. I am sure they are fine now, but as I have a system, I operate under the adage of 'if it's not broke, don't fix it.' I also look at the size of most modern welded loops and struggle to loop-to-loop 130lb zippy to my satisfaction as it is not small. I make my own braided loops from 50lb hollow braid. I fix these on both ends of the flyline, and feed the flyline up through both sections of braid before using some 10lb leader material to nail knot it down in two spots before covering the whole thing in Stormsure wonder repair liquid rubber. I then pull that through some paper to ensure the Stormsure penetrates the braid. Having set for 24 hours, it bonds the braid directly to the flyline and makes a connection stronger than the original flyline. In 15 years I have never had one fail, and some of them have survived being ripped through coral to land the fish.

James Christmas advocates a loop made from binding the end of the fly line to itself using two nail knots of 80lb braid butted against each other. The braid bites through the coating resulting in potentially the strongest loop of all. It is also advisable to make a loop large enough to pass a fly through allowing quick change of leaders on the flats.

LEADERS

This is normally the part of a book that we get into all kinds of complicate leader builds with bimini twists, class tippets and different lengths of breaking strains to create the perfect taper. Not so with GT fishing: keep it simple and brutal. I use a leader of approximately 9ft in length which is level 130lb Suffix Zippy. You will see most GT fishermen carrying a large spool of maybe two strengths. In my opinion there is no room for IGFA-type rigs in this kind of fishing as your class tippet is going to get smashed. This is not fair on the fish. I might go as low as 80lb in certain flat calm conditions or if I have had a number of flies refused, fishing in an area that has seen more anglers. Some use fluorocarbon leader material, but as long as the leader you are using is nice and supple I don't think it is really necessary to go to the added expense. Fluorocarbon material requires much more care taken over knots as it can slip and the fish don't care. Fluorocarbon also sinks which can be a disadvantage when fishing NYAPs and in the surf.

Tightening with pliers

I can hear you saying to yourself that this is a little bit overkill, but I can assure you it is not. It is not only the strength and attitude of the fish you are trying to land, but also the environment that you are trying to achieve it in. GTs like to hunt in turbulent water, normally amidst razor-sharp coral heads and they will often run straight for the drop-off. The principal reason for using leaders this brutal is abrasion resistance and if fishing a drop-off consistently such as in Sudan I will go up to 150lb. If a GT decides it is going to eat a fly, there is normally very little to deter them and they are not leader-shy. However, they don't like wire, and I have seen that refused.

On one end of this leader a single surgeon's loop is adequate provided it has been tightened with spit and pliers with the loop around a hook of some kind. I normally attach the fly so it swims on a loop of line with a combination of an improved perfection loop and a Duncan loop. So far I have not had one fail on me, but make sure that it is tightened with a pair of pliers. Simple as that.

EQUIPMENT

Because much of this fishing is done while walking significant distances in fairly deep water and getting drenched in surf, think 'less is more'. At the end of the day you have to carry it. If you are fishing with a guide then they can carry some of it, but I like to be self-sufficient so that I can take off in a direction if an opportunity arises.

The first thing you will find useful is a waterproof backpack of some kind. I have long since dispensed with a flats pack and only carry a backpack now. There are many on the market, but make sure you select one of between 20 and 30 litres which is more than enough. I would recommend a style that has a roll top rather than a watertight zip, simply as they tend to last longer. This may need a little modification if you decide that the addition of a rod holder on the opposite side you cast would be useful. A rod carrier can very easily be added by stitching a web loop to the bottom of the strap and then having a quick-release strap on the grab handle. The butt of the spare rod can be inserted into the loop and then the clip looped around it. With a little practice you will find you can switch rods quickly without removing the back pack.

Water is an essential commodity on the flats and many of those fishing in this harsh environment do not drink enough. I like to have a camelback-style hydration bladder in my backpack as I find if I have the tube on my left shoulder strap, I do actually drink from it. If you are feeling crafty, a small plastic compression fitting can be punched through just above the shoulder strap, allowing a watertight seal for the drinking tube.

INSIDE THE BACKPACK

So what goes inside? On top of the hydration bladder goes a packable spray jacket for long runs on the boat or if the weather closes in. It may be the tropics, but if you are wet and it is windy, it can get cold. I then have another roll-top wet dry sack inside to carry everything else. I carry two spare flylines on quick-change Omnispool Switchboxes in case the line is cut. These cheap plastic line boxes have revolutionised how I store my lines. Not only are they light but make switching lines in a pitching boat or stood in the middle of a flat relatively easy. A leader kit containing spare 50lb braided loops, wire threader, spool of 10lb leader, nippers and super glue for emergency repairs. Spare Polaroid sunglasses with sunrise lenses for changes in visibility. 'Happy glasses' I have found can make a huge difference to spotting on cloudy days. Lens-cleaning kit with dry cloths. If you can't spot the fish, you are handicapping yourself. Two spools of leader material in 130lb and 80lb class. Boga grip for the toothy critters. Fly pack and hook hone. Extra sunblock. Mini leatherman for repairs. A decent pair of saltwater pliers is a must for rigging, and sometimes for releasing fish. Pliers are expensive so make sure that they are attached to their case with some kind of lanyard. Finally, if you are inclined, a DSLR camera in its own waterproof bag wrapped in a small towel.

On the outside of my pack I carry a spare rod fully built and rigged, my waterproof camera on a carabiner and forceps easily accessible on the left shoulder strap. The right strap I keep completely clear in case a flyline decides to bounce and do a wrap.

CLOTHING

The environment that you will be fishing in is incredibly harsh. It is extremely hot, semi-submerged and often amidst areas of sharp broken coral. It is necessary to protect yourself from the elements. Start with a good hat, preferably something with a good brim that will help cut out the glare over the top of your glasses and help you in spotting. Some like the wide brim Tilly style hat, others baseball caps. I like a mesh back cap that allows plenty of ventilation and keeps my head cool but also dries out rapidly if submerged. I also prefer one with a dark-under brim which helps to reduce glare. Modern flats clothing is built for the job, normally impregnated with SPF 50, vents in the right places, and is quick drying.

Shirts have moved on from the cotton style with bulging pockets on the chest to a fully synthetic long tee-shirt style. Columbia, Patagonia, and a couple of others make top quality shirts. I particularly like a brand called Breathe Like A Fish from Florida. These not only have a built-in buff with a breath hole that stops your glasses steaming up, but they also have mesh down the sides and under arms. They are well-vented and I find them extremely comfortable.

A buff is a must to anyone on the flats these days. This tube of thin material can be pulled up over the nose and under the glasses and actually covers your entire face during the heat of the day. The cover also fills the gap under your glasses and when it is really bright, it aids with spotting.

Lycra shorts are essential. When up to your waist in saltwater all day, and walking distances, the lycra prevents chafe. Those who prefer to wear trousers instead of shorts for sun protection might find that they drag a lot on long wades. Full-length Lycra tights can solve this issue. The Lycra protects the legs from coral and does not drag when wet wading. The best variety are called 'jammers' which are actually designed for swimming and have built-in sun protection.

In an ideal world, the colour of your clothing should be drab, as some guides have witnessed fish spooking from unnatural colours. However, I confess I can't help myself choosing bright colours in the tropics.

Boots are crucial. The neoprene wet-suit bootie type of wading boot simply won't cut it in the surf line as the sharp coral will shred them and, by default, your feet. The last thing you want is coral in your foot as it can cause a very nasty infection. The best kind are the full-on hiking boot style of boot such as the Simms flats sneaker, Patagonia Marlwalkers or the new Orvis high leg. Another important consideration when it comes to boots is to prevent coral and sand entering your boots, so a neoprene sock with neoprene gravel guard over the top is the way forward. Simms recently introduced a combined neoprene wet wading sock and gravel guard which are excellent, extremely comfortable and protect your ankles from coral.

GLASSES

Without the ability to see your quarry, you may as well have stayed at home. Investing in really good polarised lenses is worth the money and can make a huge difference. When choosing glasses, ensure they fit your face well and do not let in too much light around the outsides. In an ideal world it is advisable to have a couple of different tints for different light conditions. In really strong light a grey-based lens will stop you squinting. In low light conditions, a bright sunrise lens is excellent. If you are only going to have one pair, then opt for an amber-based lens which performs well in both. I am a huge fan of Costa blue mirror 580 for bright conditions and liken them to HD for your eyes. There is no doubt they have aided me in spotting fish that I would have not have seen otherwise.

PACKING FOR A TRIP

I know that packing advice seems like an odd thing to find in a book about GT fishing, but there are very few GT destinations that do not require an international flight. Travelling with the right kit is key to a successful trip and the restrictions imposed after 9/11 travelling with fishing tackle are very different to how it once was. It is often necessary to contend with charter aircraft which have a limited weight allowance, sometimes as little as 15kg. Under these circumstances, packing for a trip has become a science.

Just before the luggage restrictions came in, mid-2000s, more was the way forward, having a large rolling duffle bag stuffed to the limits with every piece of tackle. I bought one of the Simms rolling duffle bags just before restrictions changed and, when full, it weighed 45kg! Your choice of bag is very important as many of the purpose-built rolling duffle bags weigh 5kg before you even put anything in them. Now I only use soft-sided duffle bags, normally of the waterproof variety, somewhere in the 90 litre category. The roll tops are excellent, but very difficult to secure. I now use overboard, North Face or my current bag is an excellent one from Fishpond.

The days of taking our precious rods as carry-on luggage are long since past, because they might be used as a 'deadly weapon'. Therefore all rods have to go in the hold and it is important to make sure they are secure and safe. I find they fit nicely inside my duffle bag, but rather than use the aluminium tubes which again weigh a lot, I have a fantastic rod case based on two lengths of square PVC drain pipe encased in cordura. I find I can easily put four rods top-and-tailed in here and normally always carry a spare 12 weight. This drops in the bottom of the bag. The next item that goes in are wading boots. These go flat on the base on one side of the rod case with my rain jacket in the space between them. They then offer protection to the kit I place on top.

When it comes to clothes, less is more. Most operations can offer laundry service these days. I normally travel with five flats shirts, two pairs of flats shorts, one pair of long Lycra tights in case I get burned and two pairs of Lycra shorts. Two pairs of socks or one pair of neoprene gravel guard combo, and two buffs, complete my fishing clothing. I will then take a few shirts, a pair of three-quarter length trousers or linen slacks for the evening and a pair of crocs for slopping around in. I pack all clothing into mesh bags as I have found compartmentalising inside my bag makes packing so much easier and cuts down on bulk. This goes in one side of the bag on top of the boots and rod case.

All my reels, loose flies, spare lines on Omnispool Switchboxes, leader material and lose metal tooling like forceps goes into a reel brief. Again this keeps it all contained and protected. This tucks into the other side. Fly pack, fly boxes and sunglasses all go in a waterproof stuff sack in the middle. Sponge bag goes on top of that in the middle to protect it, and then a couple of shirts on top complete packing.

My waterproof backpack doubles as my hand luggage. It is very sensible to have a change of flats clothing in your hand luggage along with cap and sunglasses. If for some reason your beloved luggage does not turn up at the other end, most operations can source you tackle to get you on the flats, but clothing is tricky and personal. If you can get your flats boots in, so much the better, but I am normally travelling with camera equipment and computer equipment so this has to take precedence. I find this normally weighs in at 15kg and is easily enough for a week's fishing.

The end of the road

CHAPTER 7 - FLY SELECTION FOR GTs

Which fly we cast at the fish is the most important aspect of our equipment. After all, that is the only part of our equipment the fish actually sees. There are literally thousands of fly patterns, all undergoing constant evolution, as guides and anglers tweak and adapt them to give them an edge or suit a particular area or condition they are fishing. That is one of the most wonderful things about flyfishing. Over the years I have come to realise that a really hungry GT on the hunt is very likely to snaffle most patterns that are presented correctly. The factor that influences this the most is fishing pressure. GTs, as I have touched on earlier, although predatory, are not stupid. They learn: and in areas they come into contact with fishermen on a regular basis, fly patterns need to be constantly updated and sizes of flies adapted. In the early days of GT fishing in the Indian Ocean, large crab flies adapted from permit flies were successful. After a few seasons the fish switched off those patterns. It was almost as if they had discussed it with each other. As with all flyfishing, when fish have seen a lot flies, go down in size.

Fly patterns have come a very long way from the yesteryear baitfish patterns like Bucktail Sea Habits or tarpon flies pressed into service. There has been a huge leap forward in synthetic materials now utilised in fly tying. Fly tying is the fastest-growing area in development of our sport today, from GT patterns down to tiny midges. The benefits are that large-profile flies can be built from synthetic fibres that do not absorb water but can still be cast easily. Epoxy-covered holographic eyes can now be built into patterns that give them incredible realism. UV-cured varnishes and flexible substances have made five minute epoxy nearly obsolete allowing fly tier's to be only limited by their imagination.

GT flies fall into three categories: surface flies, streamers and dredging patterns. These fish have massive mouths and they engulf large prey such as whole fish, or even birds. There was a pet GT on Alphonse Island in the mid-2000s called Whitefin which was fed a whole chicken at Christmas by the then-manager Vaughn Driessell. They like a mouthful, so patterns with a big profile are going to work well. Most GT flies are tied on 6/0 or 8/0 hooks and are some five to eight inches in length. Large eyes are attractive as they are a focus point for the fish, a little like a

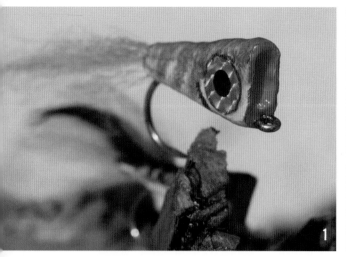

hotspot on a trout pattern. Flies are not only tied on hooks this size for the length of the pattern but also for the gape size. A large gape is key as it gains purchase in that bucket mouth.

As with all flies, favourites come and go as new patterns are developed and fish become familiar with older patterns. In the early days, round poppers from bluewater flies were pressed into service. Although the takes can be phenomenal, poppers come with their own issues, namely – it is hard to hook fish on them. A big attacking fish can push the fly away with its bow wave and miss the fly. They also tend to be tied on long-shanked hooks which can give the fish extra leverage during a fight, leading to loses. Gurgler patterns have also been used which are probably more effective. Gurglers are another surface fly made with a large piece of ether foam tied backwards and then bent forward to the eye. The ether foam protruding forward creates a substantial wake, and gurglers have traditionally been used for predatory freshwater species such as pike and taiman.

The **NYAP (1)** (Not Your Average Popper) has replaced most traditional poppers in the GT hunters' arsenal. This ingenious creation from James Christmas on Alphonse Island took the best parts of a streamer and a popper and combined them, resulting in a flat-sided streamline head that is easy to cast, but still creates plenty of disturbance to attract fish in the surf or murky water. In the surf they are particularly effective as the fly does not get caught on coral in the rolling waves which can be very irritating. There are still very few things as exciting as watching a fish explode on a popper on the surface.

The first time I fished one in anger was on Farquhar Atoll in the Seychelles after I had seen James at the landing strip waiting to depart. He had been looking after some South African clients the week before my group arrived, so it was a little like a meeting of spies as he pressed a pack of 'special flies' into my palm. I put a NYAP on, the following day, and as I moved through the surf on the edge of the atoll off 'First Island' I immediately noticed how easy it was to fish. I was

speculatively throwing a few casts off the edge of the ridge on the outgoing tide when suddenly, out of nowhere, a streak of grey and – bang! Spray, flash, grab and that fish tore out towards the bluewater. I parted company with that particular fish, but it immediately became apparent that fish had been attracted by the noise and had come a long way off to hit that fly.

The first time I headed out to the outer islands of the Seychelles to target GTs, specifically flashy profiles were the flies to use, and very rarely were they ever refused. They resemble many different forms of bait although originally conceived to resemble a small needle fish. Not only is it light and easy to cast due to the synthetics in its body, but it is extremely durable as the head is constructed from solid epoxy. A combination of chartreuse and white or pink and white with crystal flash always seemed to work best on the flats.

Only two years later, and everyone had moved onto brush patterns. **Brush flies (2)**, or 'brushys' as we call them, were originally conceived as a baitfish pattern for tiger fish in South Africa. They are relatively simple to tie and have a large profile. A clever guide heading to the Indian Ocean upsized them and they have since become one of the staple patterns used for GTs around the world. The tail is built from whole hackles mixed with a little synthetic fibre and some flash. The brush is a very large dubbed body built from craft fur, Funky Fibre, Steve Ferrar's SF blend or Mirror Image which gives it the distinctive bulky profile and makes it surprisingly resistant to being chomped. The core is stainless steel wire so it does not corrode, and if you spin your own, you can experiment with all sorts of colour combinations. The main colour is tan, but more recently black, grey, olive and red have all been used and proved successful. I have also begun experimenting with different colour bands such as black and purple. Large holographic eyes give dimension to the fly and make the profile much more realistic. I find the brush flies work best on the flats and in and around the lagoons.

Poodles (3) are one of my favourite patterns, especially when fishing offshore rock pinnacles. Tied with hanks of synthetic fibres that are somewhat curly, they do look like some demented fly dresser has been chasing a giant poodle with a pair of scissors before turning it bald. Developed on the outer atolls, this pattern has large teddy bear eyes encased in epoxy and is normally tied in black and white with a red throat. It is a very resilient pattern and I have had great success with it. The offshore poodle as mentioned before is the same dressing but tied to a length of 8 inches on an 8/0 hook and is perfect for the really big boys that live off the edge of the reef and deep structures. If teasing over these areas then this is my go-to pattern for an intercept on the teaser as it is such a massive mouthful.

The Magnetic Minnow (4) developed by Cliff Rochester and resembling a small peacock grouper, was another of the secret pack pressed into my hand on that runway. It is a large-profile pattern in black and purple entirely made from DNA holo fusion with a very large diameter holographic eye epoxied for durability. It is a very simple pattern but the flash in the body in bright sunlight is simply stunning and gives the pattern a very lifelike sheen. Tied on an 8/0 it is a substantial mouthful, but the synthetics do not absorb water at all and it is surprisingly easy to cast.

Next in the armoury are the **Sempers (5)**, tied in olive and black. The Semper Fly was originally conceived by Bob Popovics and appears in his book *Pop Fleyes*. Although originally a striped bass pattern, it has adapted very well to GTs. The tail is built from bundles of long hackle fibres and the body is made of Marabou making it particularly mobile in the water. These flies have been exceptionally effective and are simple to tie.

As well as the NYAP, James Christmas also developed a couple of other patterns which have proved deadly. The first is the **GT Mullet (6)** which incorporates a keel system to make the fly

ride correctly, along with triggers taken from observation of the natural food species underwater. The other is the **Flaming Lamborghini (7)** which resembles red snappers and lyretail groupers found around coral heads.

A much overlooked fly I always carry on the flats is the Clouser Minnow. I prefer a sparsely-tied clouser tied on a 6/0 and find these to be excellent on the flats when targeting GTs cruising on the backs of stingrays. Although tempted by a baitfish pattern, these fish are hanging off the back of the ray to see what small crustaceans might be scared or dislodged by the rooting ray, so are expecting crustaceans not bait fish. The Clouser covers all bases in this instance and when cast onto the back of the stingray will often result in an immediate smash take, just like a permit.

Although GTs eat crabs on both the flats and swimming crabs on the edge of the reef, fishing with crab patterns I have found tricky. I have seen a number of **GT crab patterns (8, 9)** cleverly put together, from giant merkins to huge Velcro crabs with rubber bands for legs. However they feel a little like casting a baseball on the end of the line, so I have tended to bypass them for more user-friendly flies. There is one excellent pattern tied by Andrew Mayo adapted from Enrico Puglisi's Red Critter which represents a crab perfectly. It is much easier to cast and works well for GTs on rays.

A recent addition to my fly armoury is the **Gym Sock (10)**, a baitfish pattern tied for roosterfish in Baja. It's a unique hollow wing design made from super hair and peril flash with a build-up of egg yarn behind the head. This pushes the fibres out, giving it a bulky profile with very little material. These examples are tied by Alex Wilkie who adapted the colours to imitate emperors on the turtle grass and peacock groupers.

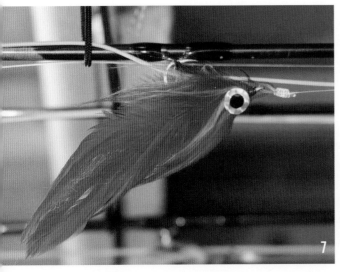

Most of these modern baitfish-profile flies are made from modern synthetics allowing easy casting. As soon as the fly is aerialised then it sloughs water off like a duck's back. When choosing which fly to fish, consider the bottom colour you will be fishing on. As a general rule, dark flies work well on dark bottoms and also in the white surf where they can easily be spotted after the wave has gone through. For light bottoms, you should choose light colours. Please also ensure you squash the barbs on all the flies you use. Not only does it penetrate better than a barbed fly, but makes releasing faster and far less damaging.

FLY STORAGE

So how do you stash 50-60 flies tied on 6/0 hooks so that the dressing is not going to be ruined? When I first started fishing these sizes of patterns, I pressed into service my normal tarpon fly boxes, usually hard-cased waterproof boxes. I realised very quickly how few patterns could be fitted in. Then someone sent me a fly wallet that contained a series of ziplock plastic bags inside and I have never looked back. These fly wallets are ideal as not only do they keep all your patterns organised and dry when totally submerged, but there are ether-foam patches on either side of the case where used flies can be stashed before you wash them out. Bonefish flies I normally throw away after a trip rather than re-use them, as they can rust in the shank under the dressing. Who wants to lose the fish of a lifetime for the sake of a few pounds? GT flies are a different story, normally tied on large shanks of metal and expensive to boot. These can very easily be washed out, dried and returned to their place. These wallets also take up a fraction of the space and weight of solid plastic boxes.

CHAPTER 8 - GT BEHAVIOUR AND HANGOUTS

So where do we find GTs? These predators are one of the most opportunistic feeders swimming in the ocean. To catch GTs on a fly you are first going to have to enter their environment and then hunt them in it. There is nothing random about how GTs move. Their movements are dictated by their unique understanding of their environment and the availability of food. And, in a similar way to humans, individual fish have their own characteristics and preferences.

Although their overriding motivation for being in a particular locale is dictated by water temperature, tide levels, available food sources and seasons, an understanding of the areas they frequent is vital. There is no quick and easy fix; it is just a question of understanding what motivates them, covering the ground and putting in the hours on the flats and the other areas they hang out. The more ground you cover and the more of their environment you can visit, the more chance you have of getting a shot. When that shot comes, you need to be ready as the opportunity comes and goes like a match lit in a wind. It can be not only physically but also mentally challenging to maintain that level of concentration for an extended period of time, often while just trying to stay upright on coral or surf.

As these bruisers are so adaptable, their hunting grounds range from offshore rock pinnacles to coral reef edges, channels, flats and estuarine systems. Juveniles tend to be more prevalent in estuaries and river systems where, like baby tarpon, they feel safe from larger predators and in turn can hunt other bait living there for the same reasons. Once they attain a certain size, perhaps 20-40cm, they will begin to group together and move out to deeper water to find structure such as a coral reef, bombies, drop-offs or channels. These locales contain strong currents where schools of bait are buffeted, making them easy targets for the fast and powerful trevally. As a rule of thumb when on the flats, the larger the group of GTs, the smaller the fish are – with the really big fish tending to remain as singles. The exception to this is a high concentration of food which will draw large concentrations of trevally to an area including the bigger fish which will shoal up again.

As soon as the tide allows, even very large GTs will venture onto flats, headlands and shallow water to hunt, utilising the network of channels or areas of deeper water. GTs can also be found along the reef edge and points where large pounding swells crash on the reef and rock, stirring up food and creating the ideal hunting ground. They will eat pretty much anything that moves or swims and are totally opportunistic. I have seen them charge packs of baitfish, tail on crabs on the flats, and I have even heard of fish along the drop-off ganging up and taking out small sharks. On Goulette island on Farquhar Atoll, the GTs have even figured out the breeding habits of the thousands of Sooty Terns that breed there. In the autumn they will track and eat a whole Sooty Tern – one innovative angler landed a GT on a 'bird fly' he had made out of a full-sized black flipflop. The GT ate it whole! For a flyfishermen, these areas of flats and coral drop-offs are the ideal place to hunt them. In an effort to bring them into some kind of order I have decided to follow the ebb and flow of a tidal cycle.

Back of the lagoon, Christmas Island

SURFING

Right at the start of the pushing tide, one of the best places to find GTs is in the surf on the reef edge on the incoming tide. The wave sets provide an ideal habitat for GTs to maraud up and down while smaller fish struggle to maintain position and balance. At low tide the front of the reef is the perfect place to start, looking in all the cuts and holes. GTs sit in these holes and wait like a trout in a stream for unsuspecting baitfish to be washed over their heads where they are easily intercepted. As the tide begins to gain momentum, the GTs become more active in their anticipation to come onto the flats. Fishermen can then move back across the coral bars as the surf increases and use the waves as windows into the world of the GT. There is nothing quite like watching a wave lift and seeing three or four GTs surfing down the inside of the wave, using the extra speed and momentum to smash into unsuspecting prey. As the angler is pushed further back from the surf line towards the shore, the GTs will gain access to the flats. It is time for the angler to move and stake out the channels that the GTs use as highways.

Surf sets on Astove Atoll, Seychelles

GT highway

CHANNELS OR GT HIGHWAYS

Channels are the first sections on the flats to become submerged and the last to lose water. All fish will generally swim in the deepest water available to them, and GTs are no exception. If you study a map of the flats you will clearly see the network of channels that resemble the veins in a leaf. Always look for intersection points from deeper water to lagoons or flats. Bonefish behave in the same way, but earlier in the tidal cycle. In lagoon systems such as Christmas Island, the GTs have preferred paths they will use to gain access to the back of the lagoon and the feeding grounds there. The same goes for flats, often large flats with depressions or channels running through them such as Orvis Flat on Christmas Island, Second Island on Farquhar or Little Snake Island in Sudan. These GT highways provide the perfect access points to the flats, just like a motorway connecting towns and cities. It can be worth staking out these highways on an incoming tide and spending a little time to see what comes along heading onto the flats. If you have the patience, you will not be disappointed.

THE FLATS

Whether it be pancake flats, turtle grass flats, coral flats or sand flats, once the water reaches critical height the GTs will slip over the edge and start to prowl like a pack of dogs, or in some cases as a lone wolf. They tend to be attracted to depressions (deeper areas within the flat), white holes and any structure that they can use as an ambush point. The great thing about having such a large fish in such shallow water is that not only can you spot them from a considerable distance if the visibility is good, but they move water, giving away their position. Always be on the lookout for bow waves, nervous water moving against the tide and also smashing of the water surface as they hunt. Keep an eye out for birds which will often track them across the flats, looking for an easy meal as the GTs stun baitfish.

Pancake flats by their very nature are an excellent hangout for GTs. Pancake flats are small hard coral flats, often covered in turtle grass, which have deep water all around them. The pancake flats inside the Christmas Island lagoon for example have long been an ideal bonefish spot, as large fish can scoot off the flat in a hurry if they become alarmed. By the same token deep water right next to shallow flats will encourage GTs to add them to their patrol route. Pancake flats inside atoll lagoons or estuaries are particularly good on dropping tides, sucking small fish off the flats much like tiger fish zoning in on bulldog baitfish on the Zambezi.

On large open flats with a combination of turtle grass and sand such as the Cosmoledo lagoon or Green Mile on Farquhar, always keep an eye out for stingrays. Like permit and bonefish, GTs like an easy meal so will follow stingrays along the flats as they grub around. Normally going dark and adopting the colour of their host, they can sometimes be hard to pick out, so if you see a stingray it's always worth a cast in their direction. These 'Ray-Rider GTs' will jump on any food item that wanders in their path. Tim Babich believes that this is a two-way relationship and the rays use the GT as an early warning device against sharks and other predators. To this end he has seen rays follow a GT after it was spooked off him, catch up with it and then begin feeding again. Although baitfish patterns remain effective, they can be refused if the GT is totally clued into the feeding of the ray in this situation – they are looking for food stirred up off the bottom by the ray. In this instance a tan Clouser or large crab pattern can be highly effective.

Green Mile, Farquhar Atoll, Seychelles

GT SNACK BARS AND BEACHES

Once the tide is reaching its full potential, baitfish are beginning to run out of cover. As before they are looking for a safe haven in shallow water, so look for the highest areas on the flats. High points such as rock piles or sand spits make ideal sheltered areas for mullet, milkfish, bones and other baitfish. Not only are they lovely spots to fish, but they can be a great area to concentrate on at high tides, as GTs will visit them for snacks. It is worth staking out these spots for a while and seeing what comes a-calling. Normally your first inkling will be a noise like a shower when the baitfish try to escape from a predator as it comes tearing in from the deeper water. Often GTs will be joined by other predatory species such as sharks, other trevally species and barracuda. They hover around on the edge of the deeper water before smashing into the bait in a feeding frenzy. Quiet beach areas where the water can be churned up also provide concentrations of baitfish.

When the tide reaches its highest point then the flats fishermen are often pushed back onto the beaches. Walking the beach edges on the inside of lagoons at this stage can be fruitful as we are not the only thing to be pushed onto the beach. Bonefish, shad and mullet will all seek the safety of the beach, so do not be surprised if gangsters come hustling down the length of sand after them. I have seen GTs hunting in packs literally chasing mullet up onto the beach in an effort to eat them and nearly beaching themselves in doing so. All that is left is blood in the water and a swirl, as the GTs depart with their meal.

CORAL ISLANDS AND OVERHANGS

At high tide GTs will forage right up against islands that were previously inaccessible to them. Baitfish will take shelter against the structure and there is always the opportunity for a terrestrial such a juicy crab or even a bird. By clambering over the top of the coral islands sometimes you will find GTs patrolling along the undercut coral or if there is fast current, even taking up station like a salmon in a stream. Cosmoledo in particular exhibits these areas and Farquhar to a lesser degree, where the sharp fossilised coral has been undercut by erosion causing the perfect chance to sneak up on a fish from above.

RIPS AND SEAMS

Continuing the logic of finding the prey and therefore finding the quarry, rips or areas of crossing currents also make ideal hunting grounds. You may find these on the ocean side of flats or on outcroppings near channels where currents are pushing in two different directions and meet. These rips make holding station extremely difficult for smaller fish species, and as a result of the cross-current, the bottom is often churned up making visibility poor. Another perfect opportunity for the mugger of the flats to pounce on unsuspecting prey. Coloured water also makes for good hunting grounds, so any area where there is sandy water on a flat that has been churned is worth throwing a fly into, to see if there is a fish hunting in there. Be speculative and you will be rewarded.

TRANSITIONAL EDGES

GTs will prowl around the edges of flats, especially if the tide has now dropped too low for them to have access. Like a GT you must cover a lot of ground to find them, but it is possible. In the back of Christmas Island lagoon there are countless sand edges dropping into deeper water.

The GTs hunt continuously, cruising tirelessly up and down these edges in their quest for food. Mullet, milkfish, goatfish and bonefish will all hide and feed in these shallow areas to escape predators and are sometimes corralled by hungry GTs.

The edges around atolls are the final spot a hungry GT can grab a meal before they are pushed off the edge of the reef by the receding water. Look for deep holes or pockets along the edge for any GTs that have taken up station – essentially the same as the beginning of the push. By ducking under the current flowing over their heads, they can use minimal energy but hammer any unsuspecting target as it is pushed over them by the current.

SHARKS

GTs exploit sharks in an interesting way by using them as moving cover. They will 'ride' sharks, which allows them to get within easy striking-distance of a potential meal. As a shark cruises along, baitfish move away without necessarily spooking, providing a prime opportunity for a GT to see food before it sees them, and grab an easy meal. Big nurse sharks are one of their favourite species to shadow and often these gentle giants have a group of GT friends playing grandmother's footsteps. Any large shark might have a little buddy, so if you see one always check it out, and if visibility is poor it is definitely worth a cast. I remember my first trip to Cosmoledo and seeing a large lemon shark cruising the flats from a distance. My guide turned round and told me to run towards it – 'Come again?' I thought, wondering if he had lost his mind. Sure enough two GTs were tail-gating him, I got a cast out and one of the fish hit the fly immediately. This is where sometimes the GT/shark relationship can be strained as the shark might then come after the hooked GT, but generally in the encounters I have had, the shark carries on its merry way.

Sharks do need to be treated with respect. If you leave them alone, then on the whole they will leave you alone and they are normally attracted by splashing and disturbance. Try and identify the species from a distance as you do not want to be running towards a tiger or bull shark on the flats. In certain cases on Farquhar I have also seen GTs over a metre long being followed around by a small shark. If you see a fin, take courage in both hands and always investigate.

White sand spit, St Brandons, Mauritius

PINNACLES

There is no place that GTs like to hang out in numbers more than rock pinnacles. Think of these as underwater mountains that reach up from the depths to become small areas of land or even remain totally submerged. The shallower water above them becomes a haven for baitfish, and often the surf and currents that these pinnacles create as the ocean passes over and around them make an ideal hunting ground for GTs. Normally pinnacles have small areas above water, sharp troughs along the beach edge that the hunters can access close to shore, along with coral flats leading to a steep drop-off. A prime example would be some of the GT haunts in Sudan where the edge drops away to 600ft or more. Unlike some edges in the Seychelles, the lack of tide and sometimes even surf allows the angler to venture right to the edge. Packs of GTs patrol routes over the top and around these pinnacles waiting for some poor unsuspecting baitfish to be swept over the edge of the shallow water into the blue where they become easy fodder. Battles in these areas can be intense as the GTs can bolt for deep water and cut you on the edge. Pinnacles, along with any other deep structure are often used as resting spots between tidal shifts.

The edge, Nubian Flats, Sudan

BOMMY BASHING

Coral heads provide a fantastic ambush site that GTs can use to their advantage. Like trigger fish they will take up station in and around these heads that smaller fish will gravitate towards as a place of security. Fish will change colour and blend with the environment making them hard to spot. Clusters of coral head or coral bommies can often be an ideal spot to target inside a lagoon system in and around the reef edge. Most GTs hiding amongst coral heads are looking for a meal. Presenting a large fly in this situation or a hookless teaser to pull the fish away from the head allowing a free cast can often produce some stunning attacks. I personally love to use a popper such as the NYAP in this situation. Bommy bashing can be an excellent location to try when many others are not firing, in the same way as pinnacles bommies are often used as a resting spot in-between tides.

Be warned: although it is often possible to find and hook a fish hunting by a coral head, hanging on to it is entirely a different story. Coral heads by their nature are sharp and a hooked GT will do its level best to knit your fly line amongst them. Fly line, leader and backing can return shredded beyond use and many fish escape. Nevertheless it is extremely exciting and that should not put you off. If you are not prepared to bleed a little equipment, then GT hunting is not for you.

TEMPERATURE

GTs like cooler water in an ideal world, but being robust they are more willing than other species to also hunt in warmer conditions. You will often be surprised by a big GT marauding down a beach edge in greenish water looking for a snack. Always be ready as they will sneak up on you when you least expect it. Water temperature is important though and sometimes when you step onto the flats and the temperature feels like bath water, it is best just to move on. GTs will hunt in that temperature, but generally bonefish and other prey species will not be found on flats that warm.

In conditions like this, which normally arise on neap tides where the water has baked in the sun, try and locate areas where cool water comes flooding into the flats system from the ocean, especially on the push of the tide.

CHAPTER 9 - TIDES

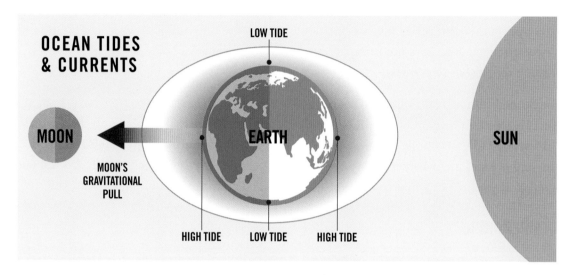

For a saltwater fisherman, tides are the key to success. If you can relate tidal movement to the area you are fishing, it allows you to figure out where the fish will be and by default how successful you will be in encountering them. If you are fishing with a guide as opposed to fishing on your own or with someone who is just handling a boat, the guide will know the area intimately and how the tides apply. To understand tides fully and how they can be used to your advantage, it is important to have a basic understanding of how they come about and factors that can affect them. The fresh clean water that an incoming tide brings refreshes the flats and breathes new life on each cycle. Water that has remained on the flats for a length of time becomes tepid or simply too hot to hold fish.

Think of the world's oceans as a rubber skin around the earth. There are two masses that can grab that rubber skin and pull on it, making it stretch on two sides, the moon and the sun. The moon creates roughly twice the pull of the sun and as it travels around the earth it causes the ocean to bulge towards it, creating high tide. As the moon also pulls the earth towards it, another high tide is created on the opposite side and leaves low tides on the remaining sides. When the sun and moon line up together this exaggerates the gravitational pull, creating spring tides which are the two larger tides of the lunar month in the weeks of the new and full moon. When the moon is at right-angles to the sun, the sun cancels out some of its gravitational pull creating the smaller or neap tides. The lunar rotation of the earth tales 24 hours and 55 minutes and is why the tides move by 55 minutes per day. As the orbit of the moon is not perfect around the earth, this can also influence the tides as the distance between the two dictates the strength of their attraction to one another, just like a magnate on a piece of metal. The closer you are, the stronger the pull. This is why full moon spring tides are marginally bigger than the new moon spring tides – on the full moon, the moon is in-between the sun and earth creating the largest effect.

As this 'wave' moves around the earth it causes currents and these in turn ebb and flow over the topography of the ocean and coastal shelves, which create delays on how the sea flows into areas of coastline. That is why some areas have one high tide a day (diurnal) and some have two high tides in a day (semi-diurnal). Other factors that influence tides are wind and barometric pressure. Strong onshore winds can 'push' the tides higher than they would normally, and also delay them being able to ebb. Strong offshore winds have the opposite effect, preventing the tide from reaching as high as predicted and also making them ebb faster than predicted. Barometric pressure has a similar effect, with low pressure creating larger tides than expected as there is less force pushing down on the oceans – whereas high barometric pressure suppress the tides. It is good to be aware of conditions and take them into account on how they will affect the tides.

So as fishermen: how do we use tides? The easiest way is to use tide charts generated by computer software which will give a certain amount of accuracy where you are fishing. Tide charts are generated using tidal stations in various parts of the world so although they can give you a rough idea, they are not gospel and are predictions based on extrapolated data. For most of our purposes though, they are good enough. A tide chart at first glance can look a little like the output of an ECG, but it is really just a correlation of water height plotted against a time axis. By knowing the approximate depths on the areas you wish to fish, it is quite simple to deduce where you need to be and when. I also should add: where *not* to be caught. A fast-rising ride is a dangerous place to be. Some atolls can have a push of as much as eight feet, which is very frightening if you do not know the area well. As the tide charts are based on certain harmonic stations, there is nothing that beats local knowledge.

For example one area on Farquhar Atoll has its high tide an hour before the chart predicts and has no slack tide at all. This is because it is the lowest part of the atoll: an example of topography affecting the tide. If I had not been fishing with a knowledgeable guide I would not have known that, and could have been caught out, a situation which could be life-threatening. A guide has spent months and years in succession on these areas so will know the idiosyncrasies of individual flats much like a salmon guide understands how the lies move with different water heights.

There is much debate as to which tides are best for GT fishing, and this of course can vary hugely from destination to destination. The first thing I find consider is: what a GT is looking for and how the tide can facilitate that. You then need to adapt that to the topography of where you are fishing. Trevally are apex predators, but also totally opportunistic. In a full tidal cycle they will wait around the edge of a reef or atoll, hunting the edges until they have enough water flowing on to the flats for them to get up into the shallow water and attack the bait there. They will spend as long hunting those fish trying to get away from them as possible, before being pushed back off the flats on the

dropping tide. By looking at a tide chart it is possible to predict when these windows of opportunity present themselves, and combining this with local knowledge of which flats appear at which stages will give you a massive advantage.

Originally it was thought that big spring tides were best for GTs with the large flow of water bringing more fish in on the push. Although action can be fast and furious, your window of opportunity can be limited to an hour or two on prime spots on the edge of an atoll before you get pushed back by the flood of water. If you are fishing without a guide, make sure the boat is never far away in these conditions.

The benefit of a big spring tide is that different areas come into play as the extra water opens new hunting grounds. For example on Christmas Island lagoon, GTs will hunt right to the back of the lagoon which for most of the Luna cycle is inaccessible to them due to water height. Don't be afraid to explore on big springs as the push hits the front line. You may find action where you least expect it along beach edges and back country areas, as the predators follow the prey.

Over the years I have come to prefer a neap tide building to a spring tide, preferably over a new moon, as this can give you the best of both worlds. There has always been some debate about the full moon as some say that fish feed under the full moon at night and therefore do not take readily during the day. I have to say I have fished both many times and have never witnessed anything to make me believe that this affects GT fishing. In an ideal world when dates are flexible then I would pick a new moon just to satisfy the 'what if?'

CHAPTER 10 - THE HUNT

ON FOOT

If you intend to hunt a predator in a foreign environment, you have to adapt. Those of us who have spent many hours wading the flats for bonefish and other species are used to being in, on, and around the saltwater habitats. Searching for GTs on the flats is perhaps the pinnacle of this style of fishing. I would rather catch one fish by hunting on foot then ten from anywhere else as it is far more rewarding. It is what sets the GT flyfisherman apart from most other methods of flats fishermen. It is hard work.

GTs will move into feeding areas, be it flat or surf zone, as soon as the water is deep enough for them to swim in. This can be in water so shallow that just their eyes are covered and a third of their body is exposed. The shallower the water, the better it is for anglers. It is far easier to move around in knee-deep water than thigh deep water and in the shallower water, it is easier to spot fish from

Watching

farther away. The GTs cone of vision is smaller in shallow water so you can narrow the distance between you with less likelihood of being spotted. Once the fish are in thigh-to-waist-deep water, they can be difficult to spot especially if they are on a turtle grass or mottled bottom flat.

Although water depth is secondary to finding the right area, anglers will sometimes find themselves in deeper water than they would hunt other species such as bonefish, and you need to be prepared for this. It is a big step moving from ankle and calf depth water to wading around in knee to mid-thigh or even waist depth, often in a fast pushing tide and stumbling over rough coral. It takes some getting used to and requires a different mind-set. As I mentioned in the introduction, my own baptism to this environment made me nervous. Other things swim in this depth of water that are also hunting and suddenly it is harder to see the bottom as often the water is turgid. However if you wish to bump into the gangster of the flats, this is where you need to be.

I liken it to the difference between driving a car and riding a motorcycle. In a car you are relatively secure, but as soon as you ride a motorcycle you are open to the environment and have to develop eyes in the back of your head as it is considerably more dangerous... But it is also far more of a rush and considerably more exciting! Those who are used to deep wading in rivers adapt quickly as you need to try and use the currents hitting your body rather than remain rigid and fight them. Move with the ebb and flow if you can and turn your body sideways to incoming waves if you are in the surf line.

Hopping as the waves hit you and averting your face will prevent continual soaking and more importantly it will keep your glasses clean so you can see. As you wade, as with the river bank, it is best to take the lowest path available between coral heads as this keeps your centre of gravity low rather than teetering higher up and trying to move from head to head. You are less likely to be sent tumbling by an unseen wave set. Continuing the car analogy, you need to be able to move in this environment without having to think about it too much so that you can concentrate on spotting fish. Keep an eye out for hazards such as sharks, sharp coral heads, rays and of course waves.

ON A BOAT

The great thing about being on a boat is vantage point. The higher you are, the further you can see. Apart from not being nearly as physical, it is also possible to cover large areas until you start seeing a few fish or hit the right depth to wade which is a distinct advantage. 'Putting along' on very slow speed of the prop can be a good way of covering large areas quickly. Be aware though that the engine noise might well raise awareness of your presence, and GTs learn fast. In the early days of the Seychelles there were instances of fish trying to eat a propeller, but now they will steer well clear of engine noise. The more aware of humans they are will dictate their reaction.

The ideal scenario would be a flats boat with a pole, but at the time of writing I don't know of any GT fishing locations that are so equipped. On most of the Indian Ocean atolls, poles are not used because the tidal fluctuation is too great. Some dedicated guides will hop over the side and become a human pole, pushing you across the flats like a king on a litter, but the disadvantage of this is that you lose their eyes as they have lost their vantage point.

Being on board a boat can also make a good casting platform as the line is not subject to resistance from surface tension of the water as it shoots. Make sure that you are ready. Have 20 yards of line stripped off and controlled. In a boat I will sometimes go barefoot as you can use your toes to manage line (but make sure you have sun block on them!) and ideally drop the line into the well as then the wind won't manage to turn your best cast into a bird's nest. A good guide will cruise around likely areas, but if there is an edge where it is likely something might happen, always encourage them to turn the engine off and drift those segments. This depends on the area being fished and the tide.

CHAPTER 11 - CAST, HOOK, STRIKE & FIGHT

As soon as you hit the flat, strip a comfortable distance of line off the reel (maybe 15 yards) and cast it out. Retrieve until you can hold the fly in your left hand (if you are right-handed: vice versa for left-handed) and still have 9-10ft out of the tip guide. Then ensure you rest the drag to prevent overrun. More fish are lost like this than any other error. Trail the remainder in the water behind you, as you wade. If you are wading across a current, ensure the line is hanging on the unfettered side. This is the same as the ready position when tarpon fishing. From here one can very rapidly throw a loop, load the rod and cast that fly out to the fish as fast as possible. Check that your line is clear from time to time, as it can twist. If it becomes stuck on a piece of coral *do not* be tempted to pull it free, but retrace your steps and carefully unhook it. This is not some undergrowth on a riverbank but probably razor sharp coral, quite capable of nicking your line and at worse cutting into the core.

THE CORE

When it comes to casting, numerous books go into huge amounts of detail and far more eloquently than I could. If you have fished for tarpon before and you are comfortable on the bow of a skiff casting at tarpon using a 12#, do not think it will be the same when GT fishing on foot. Whilst on the bow of that skiff you were two feet above the water, you had a balanced leader on the end of the fly line, typically quite thin, and you were casting a very light 1/0 fly. The key point is that casting an 11# or 12# fly rod with a 475 grain fly line, 130lb leader and something the size of a small chicken on the end whilst standing in knee-to-thigh-deep water is not easy. Your line is travelling closer to the water, while the fly and leader are heavier and more wind-resistant. This means less line speed, better timing to load the rod and when you shoot the line it sticks to the water surface and gets sucked by the current. It is considerably more difficult than casting to a tarpon from a flats skiff.

For most flyfishers who are proficient with smaller line classes, it takes a lot of practice to feel comfortable with that rig in your hand, so if you have not done a lot, ensure you practice before your trip and not on the flats when you have a yard-long GT cruising toward you. I would also recommend that you become proficient at backhand casting. Invariably that GT is going to appear on your wrong shoulder or across the wind, and a backhand cast will enable you to deliver a rapid presentation without burying a 6/0 hook in the back of your head. With a 12# set-up this is one of the most useful casts in your armoury and in some ways is easier than casting forehand, especially if you have weaker wrists. The butt of the rod can be pressed into the forearm and provide a secure point to bend the rod tip, making it do the work rather than your arm. The better you can cast, the more opportunities you will be able to take advantage of. Sometimes these are few and far between, so don't fluff them because your casting is not up to scratch. Do you need to be able to cast a brushy 45 yards backhand across the wind to catch a GT? No, but you should to be able to double haul it 20 yards into the wind. As with driving a car, there is enough going on around you that requires your attention than concentrating on how to physically drive it. Flats fishing is the same: if your casting is proficient then you can focus on the environment around you such as the surf, coral heads and other hazards that are hard enough to keep track of at the best of times.

So you have put the time in, waded across the flats, walked the surf line, and suddenly – out of the blue – materialises a big GT cruising in your direction. What happens next? Be still the beating heart, the first thing to go through your head should be speed. Cast the fly out in the vicinity of the fish as fast as possible and make your first cast your best. Above all things when flyfishing for GTs it is this moment that counts. Those who can capitalise on the opportunities when they come are going to be more successful. These marauders of the flats can come and go like a breath of wind. The hard part when you are walking the flats is to maintain that level of concentration and to be ready for the shot. I have on numerous occasions witnessed fellow anglers wading the flats carrying a rod tucked under their arm with the fly still on the ring. There is no way that a fish is going to hang around while the angler takes the fly off the ring, strips some line off the reel and prepares to make a cast.

WORKING THE FLY

When it comes to placing the fly in relation to the cruising fish, in an ideal world you need to pull the fly directly away from it, as GTs like to run their food down. The fly should come off at an angle from the direction the fish is travelling, and not too acutely. Fleeing prey brings out their aggressive instincts and will often spur them into attack. They are not keen on flies swimming toward them, as they probably don't encounter too many baitfish trying to commit suicide. This unnatural action might spook them.

One of the worst angles to deal with is when the fish is coming straight at you. I remember an instance when I was wading up from the ocean side in a dropping tide and checking holes near a large channel. Sure enough I found a big GT hanging just off the current waiting for a meal. I provided one in the form of a small grey brushy mullet. I dropped the fly just to one side of its nose. As the current took hold of the line I began to strip and the fish charged round straight toward me. As its eyes came above the water and it engulfed the fly it was moving so fast that it was impossible to maintain contact. Strip striking was challenging and I failed to hook it. If you can manoeuvre to gain better angle then do so: if not, take the shot anyway but as soon as the fly lands maintain contact so that you can strike effectively.

Casting flies at these fish is not like dry flyfishing – a silky presentation is not paramount. I firmly believe that GTs are not as fussy as tarpon, for example. If they are in attack mode I have seen a fish charge down a fly landing 20ft away before the angler even had time to sort out slack line and start retrieving. Often dreadful turnovers of the cast can almost be more effective. If there is more than one fish, they will compete for the fly. In fact I will often slap the fly down on the water just to attract attention. You should try to read the body language of your target though. If the GT is static in a tidal stream, for example, then a fly drifted through its vision on a swing will be more effective. Factors that should be considered when presenting the fly are: the depth of water the fish is sitting in; the power of the current that will grab the line and control the speed of the drift; whether the fish is cruising or stationary; and how aggressive it appears to be. It is possible to read the body language of a fish to give you an idea of its frame of mind. If a GT is stationary in the current, but moving furtively from side to side like a trout in a stream, then it is most likely going to be hot.

Not all GTs eat the fly. Just because they are an apex predator and a swimming dustbin does not mean they will charge and eat every fly presented to them. I often find it odd when fishermen remark on this. For all you know it might have eaten a whole mullet 10 minutes ago and be digesting. These disinterested fish can sometimes be made to eat a 'wafer-thin mint' if the fly is presented carefully and 'fed' to it. A fly dropped quite close and pulsed can stimulate a strike. However GTs can become nervous in certain water heights and tidal stages and the way the fish is moving across the flats will give you an idea as to its mood. If the fly is rejected it could be the way you fished the fly.

Once you have landed the fly, if you are able, let it sink. I think this is one of the most common faults and one I know I have been guilty of on numerous occasions. If you have led the fish far enough you need to let the fly get down to eye level. Wait for the fish to see the fly before you start stripping. If the fish doesn't pick up on it, give it one slow strip to just draw its attention. Hold the rod out in front of you, not tucked into the body. If you can, strip automatically then watch the fish, but otherwise watch where you are grabbing the line from. If the fish hits straight away you still then have the distance of one strip to set the hook. The moment he sees it you will see a change in body language and you can start speeding up the strip. If you start the strip too soon you will pull the fly out of his cone of vision and he won't see it. A GT is not trout looking up through a conical window for a dry fly: its eyes converge forwards on the plane it is moving on. It does however have slightly convex eyes, giving it a wider field of vision. If you start stripping the fly as soon as it lands, quite often the fly will look unnatural and skip across the surface. Flies with plenty of dressing will look more realistic when saturated and travelling on a lower plane. A fast long strip of about 1½-2ft is normally the best way to provoke a reaction, speeding up as the fish chases. Do not stop the strip or it is likely the fish will lose interest. GTs are used to seeing baitfish swim for their lives away from them.

If you are fishing with a NYAP or other kind of popper, then point the rod at the water and as you strip with one hand you should move the rod the same distance with the other hand in a Y-shaped motion while moving the tip. This effectively doubles the strip length and will create the maximum amount of disturbance for the least amount of effort. Stripping poppers for an extended length of time if you are searching an area can be tiring and this technique will conserve you energy over a one-handed strip and make the popper push more water. However you must be careful not to over-extend the rod too much to the side. If you then have a take at close range you will not be able to use it to help drive the hook home.

THE STRIKE

As soon as the fish takes, grab the line, point the rod straight at it and yank the line back or 'strip strike' as hard as you can two or three times. Then concentrate on controlling the line and getting it on the reel as quickly as possible. Never try and 'trout strike' and set the hook with the rod. You cannot generate enough pressure to set the hook and it is highly likely the two of you will part company. If in doubt or if you have run out of line to strip, run backwards while continuing to point the rod straight at the fish. If you try and set the hook sideways, you will lose the power as the rod bends. Loose line is a recipe for disaster and will immediately wrap itself round the rod butt, reel handle, your finger (painful!) or anything else it can find. There can be very few things in the fishing world as awe-inspiring as a GT charging down a fly. It's like watching a jet fighter hit the afterburner as it accelerates to ludicrous speed. The fish then planes up in the water like a submarine blowing its ballast tanks and that bucket mouth opens engulfing anything in its path. As it surfaces, most of its head clears the water and often you have sense of being eyeballed. It is a sight that keeps me awake at night. The only thing that beats a GT attacking a fly is a *bunch* of GTs attacking the fly. In the early days on Cosmoledo in the Seychelles we would have gangs of fish tearing around our ankles. I remember seeing one fish hit my fly and as I tried to catch up with it, two more were trying to eat the fly out of the side of its mouth!

Full curvature of the rod

FIGHTING A GT ON A FLY ROD

I learned the secret to fighting these terrors of the flats from one of the best, Andrew Parsons, in Mozambique many moons ago. Andrew was the father of coastal GT fishing there and his philosophy is to 'give that fish horns'. For those not familiar with this expression, when translated from South African fish-speak (yes, it is a language, I have checked) it means 'hook and hold'. If you give a GT an inch in a fight it will take a yard, not unlike a tuna in blue water. You have to crush its spirit in the first five minutes by giving it everything you have got. What ensues is really a tug of war.... and the odds are pretty even.

In real terms this means: give it as little line as possible. Pump and wind, constantly changing the angles on the fish by pulling in the opposite direction of travel with the rod at the side of the body. Keep the rod low and lean back using the whole curvature of the blank, employing as much of the power in the butt section as possible. Never move the rod above 45 degrees or you will lose purchase. There is no room for a trout high stick here or they will quite simply destroy you and your gear by ripping the line straight through the nearest coral bommy. On the flats I also like to use Billy Pate's famous 'low blow' style he developed for tarpon. As the fish swims away, pull its head down into the flat while also knocking it off balance. The battle can turn out to be an even fight as the GT can go side up and use its surface area as a drogue while swimming around you in circles.

This style of battle has casualties, normally lines and rods, but occasionally anglers. While fishing off the Astove channel in the Seychelles a few years back, myself and a couple of other intrepid anglers smashed four rods and cut three lines in a little over two hours. One rod smashed itself into seven pieces and we had to cut it off the line to conclude the battle. Each fish that came out of the channel was over 100lb. I began to wince every time we hooked up, as we knew something was going to break. We landed one we estimated at 120lb and a fork length of 136cm. It was carnage!

LANDING AND RELEASING

Once you have managed to fight the fish to a standstill, check where the hook hold is, first and foremost. You will find a lot of good guides will try and get out to the fish and get a hand to it before it starts thrashing around in shallower water where it might damage itself or attract unwanted attention from other predators. This is a crucial stage as the last thing we wish to do is damage these majestic creatures. Ideally, you have been using a barbless hook which causes less physical damage and also eases the hook removal, even if it is buried deep. Some believe that barbless hooks result in fewer fish landed, while others appreciate the challenge and value causing less hooking damage to these epic beasts. I actually believe that a barbless hook penetrates better, giving you a more solid hook hold.

The best way to handle GTs is to grab the leader and then get a grip of the base of the tail (or caudal peduncle). Once you take away his motor, he is a bit stuck. But be warned, the caudal peduncle has sharp scutes on it so a glove is necessary to hold it securely and prevent cutting up your palm. Bradley Hyman once described these fish as being the 'high school bullies' in that once you get hold of them they actually give up. Unlike a tuna or a bonefish, a GT tends to lie relatively still while you slip the hook out. This is probably due to the exhaustive fight. If there is a tidal current, make sure to hold the GT face-first into the flow of water. In general, a fish's gills only work if water is flowing in the mouth and out the gill flats (or operculum). Gills do not work if a fish is moved backwards in the water – it is actually counterproductive for the fish in terms of reviving it from the fight. They may be big, brutish fish, but nevertheless they need to be treated with respect and care.

Nine times out of ten they are hooked in the corner of the jaw or somewhere around the jaw line due to the nature of the take. However, occasionally they take it deep into the gill rakes, and in this instance the best thing to do is to cut the fly off the leader. If the fly is easily accessible from the gill plate and there isn't excessive bleeding, *very* gently insert a pair of pliers in through the gill plate and gently remove the hook backwards. Never put your hand inside a GTs mouth unless you wish for some nasty puncture wounds to your wrist. If the hook is deeply-lodged in any part of the mouth or oesophagus, it is better to cut the line and leave the hook in place rather than digging around vital organs, such as the gills.

Measuring in the water

GIANT TREVALLY MEASUREMENT TO WEIGHT RATIO

Length (CM)	Weight in lbs.
60	9.8
65	12.5
70	15.6
75	19.2
80	23.3
85	28
90	33.2
95	39
100	45.5
105	52.7
110	60.6
115	69.3
120	78.7
125	88.9
130	100.1
135	112
140	125
145	138.8
150	153.7

Never lift a GT by its tail upside down or you can damage the spine, and never lift one by a Boga grip in the mouth. The best way to judge the size of a GT is measure its length with a tape measure. This is where you will hear the phrase 'fork length' which is the measurement from the snout horizontally along the lateral line to the point of the tail where the fork meets. This is the correct measurement and there are various algorithms for calculating the weight from this figure. As soon as you land the fish, quickly measure it. When it comes to lifting for a picture, keep the fish in the water while you and the person with the camera get prepared. Always let the person with the camera call the shots. On three, lift and click. The GT should not be out of the water for more than 10-15 seconds; however it is even better not to air expose the fish at all. Fish do not breathe out of water and air exposure after angling only increases the recovery time. If you must get a picture with your prize GT, lift it quickly when the person with the camera says 'Now'. Support the GT with one hand under the chest near the pectoral fins and the other around the base of the tail. If you want to reposition for another photo, put the fish back in the water until you and the person with the camera are all set up. The prime rule is to never leave the fish out of the water for any longer than strictly necessary.

When reviving the GT, pay attention to whether there are coordinated movements of the fins. If you loosen up your grip and the fish even slightly rolls to one side or the other, hang on to it a little longer. If there is a current, hold the fish with its head pointed into the flow. If your GT is really showing signs of fatigue, consider walking it on the flats or moving it in a figure-of-eight pattern to help get more water flowing over the gills. If your GT is looking strong with fins moving well and the eye wanting to check you out, then slowly let go and watch your GT-memory swim away. Do keep an eye on it as long as you can, just in case it does need a bit more care. There is nothing quite like seeing one slide back into the water and swim away to grow bigger. Take a moment of calm after the battle, as catching a GT on a fly is difficult – you have achieved greatness.

Strong release

CHAPTER 12 - SPOTTING & WEATHER

The great thing about GTs is they are big fish. Much like looking for tarpon on the flats, if there is a GT within eyesight you are most likely going to see it, provided you are concentrating. Unlike bonefish which vanish as soon as they turn sideways due to their reflective scales, GTs are almost too big to hide. As you move across the flats you should scan in a systematic manner. Move your head and eyes from left to right in a 180 degree arc. We all end up developing what I call the 'Cosmoledo' sweep which is as your eyes scan from left to right every third sweep, look behind you. You never know what might be playing grandmothers' footsteps. While wading out from Depose island on Farquhar to a rock pile with Tim Babich, we were so focused on what was in front of us we did not notice that the noise of our wading and scrunching had attracted a massive GT that had come sliding in behind us to investigate if we might be worth eating.

They tend to catch you unawares by the speed they move. You look one way, scan, and when you have scanned back again suddenly they are in your window of sight. In good visibility GTs normally appear a grey-blue colour as they cruise the flats, although sometimes they are black and very easy to spot. As with all spotting on the flats, the usual tricks apply: concentrate on looking for movement. In a current or on the edge of a flat, look near the edge or coral bommies where they will hold station waiting for prey. Here a slight movement or dart to intercept prey can give away their position. Every time you see a ray or a shark, let your eye linger longer to see if they have friends joining them.

Birds can often betray the presence of a GT. Birds are the fisherman's signpost and by keeping a close eye on the natural wildlife around you and their reaction to the environment, you will learn a lot. Most bird species living in these areas are piscivores and are far better at this than we are. Although this comes as second nature to bluewater fishermen who use the birds to show them the location of schools of bait or bait being pushed to the surface by predators underneath, we often overlook these indicators on the flats. Look for gulls or terns ducking up and down over an area of flats as this is where the baitfish will have congregated and GTs are sure to be in the vicinity. It's also worth looking high up as some of these predatory birds have magnificent eyesight and you will see them flying in tight circles over bait. On the flats, herons are one of the greatest hunters of all and will show you for sure where the bait is hiding. By concentrating on these birds you can cut down on some searching, as those with far keener eyesight and instincts have done the hard work for you.

We all hope that when we head for the tropics the weather will be superb and that visibility will be outstanding all week. Good light is extremely helpful when spotting fish on the flats and can light up hundreds of metres in every direction, making the task at hand considerably easier. However, when the weather does not go your way, it is vital not to just give up. Wading on the flats in bad light, drizzle or strong wind can be challenging, but by no means impossible. The first aid is different coloured lenses in your glasses. Always have a pair of sunrise lenses for bad light conditions, it makes a huge difference.

If light conditions are not favourable then move really slowly. If it is simply a cloud coming across the sun then stop until your light comes back. If it is a case of overcast skies then reduce your pace dramatically. The slower you move, the more likely you are to pick up on signs around you and it will prevent you from stepping on fish. Spooking fish at your feet can be extremely frustrating.

If you can find an area of light bottom to wade on, preferably sand flats, it is easier to spot moving fish. If there are dark bars across these lighter flats, this can also help as the contrast makes it easier to see movement. Ideal areas are ridge lines where there are two contrasting colours, making it easier to notice a fish as soon as it moves onto light coloured bottom.

On a dropping tide, look for white holes near the edge of the flats on the lagoon side or ocean side, or the edge of the flats as the tide comes off. Often GTs will find a spot that they can sit under the current and just hoover up unsuspecting bait fish as they are swept off in the fast currents. Normally these areas are lighter in colour and can make spotting possible.

One of the biggest lessons to learn in poor light conditions is to stop looking *into* the water and start looking *at* the water. With our superb polaroid glasses these days we have all been accustomed to being able to spot fish in the water at great distances. However this was not always the case and fishermen of yesteryear had to rely far more on instinct for locating their quarry. Once you concentrate your attention on the surface, look for anything that does not look right. When the tide is moving across a flat, GTs (and most other species for that matter) tend to hunt up-tide. As they move against that current their body will betray them. Dancing or 'Nervous Water' can be the first indicator. In the case of GTs you will often see a bow wave in shallow water as a fish that size moving across a flat cannot conceal itself that well. Keep an eye out for tips of

Perfect spot to see fish coming onto the flat

GT fin

dorsal fins, tails, and unusual baitfish movements. Birds can be an indicator of a GT using the bad light to hunt down prey.

Makes sure you put out blind casts around you as you wade. The sound of your wading can often attract a GT and you will pick up fish in your vicinity. Poppers like NYAPs are ideal for this as they create surface disturbance and bring the fish to you rather than you to them. I have relished picking up a few fish on poor visibility days and turned a tough day into a success.

I remember one day on Cosmoledo where the light had been bleak all day with intermittent rain storms. We had waded for miles across some deeper flats. My arm was beginning to ache a little from the 'ready' position in which I was carrying the rod. As I was Tail End Charlie on the wading line, I started throwing blind casts out around me. At that point I really was not expecting to catch anything, but the thing about not being able to see the fish is that they can't see you either. As I stripped the fly in while looking in another direction, there was a small explosion as a GT came out of nowhere and smashed the flashy profile I was fishing with. I freely admit to screaming like a girl as it took me by surprise, but luckily due to the direction of the wind I don't think anyone heard me.

Where applicable, using a teasing plug can also locate fish and bring them to you. This is not a technique I advocate for the flats as over-use can be detrimental to a GT population who become wise to it quickly. However if you are fishing along the reef edge at low tide, I do not think it does any harm if sight fishing is not an option.

CHAPTER 13 - OFFSHORE AND BLUEWATER GT FISHING

When you find that either the flats are not firing or there is too much or too little water on them, sometimes looking for offshore areas of rock pinnacles, ridges or even the drop-off can be very productive for GTs. Occasionally you come across an ecological phenomenon such a swimming crab migration occurring that can look like an oil slick oozing off the side of an atoll, and when this occurs you can either go and hunt other flats species or you can follow them into the bluewater. These areas of structure form their own eco-systems of baitfish and predators, GTs amongst them. From a flyfishing perspective, there are two methods of getting at these fish holding in deeper water: teasing and dredging. A fish finder can be very helpful here to pinpoint the structure so that you can time the cast and direct it accordingly.

Teasing the blue

TEASING

Tease and switch technique is just like sailfishing, although drifting rather than trolling. Your boat partner or guide will throw out a hookless popper or pencil plug such as a 'GT Ice Cream' over the structure you have identified. Having cast it out to cover the structure, the rod is then kept high and the teaser is reeled back, skittering across the surface and creating lots of disturbance. This style of locating fish can be very exciting as they will hit the lure at full pace and attacks will be fast and furious; often a massive explosion of white water as the fish hammer it. I remember on Farquhar watching a pack of GTs come out of nowhere off a rock pinnacle and the largest must have been about 1½m and quite frankly, it scared us with the way it hit the plug. The person on the teaser then attempts to keep the fish's interest and tease it to the boat where the flyfishermen can make a cast. It is vital to begin casting well before the teaser makes it within casting shot. The teaser is then yanked out and the angler drops the fly in the spot that the now-confused and really amped fish is. Just like an angry sailfish, the GT will hammer the fly and serious battle will commence. It is often around these pinnacles that some of the largest GTs live, so be prepared with the correct tackle as there are often casualties.

DREDGING

The other option is to dredge, the technique developed in Mozambique by Andrew Parsons. A very fast-sinking line is twinned with a heavily weighted fly such as an 8/0 mega clouser with very large lead eyes. Again the best spots for this style of fishing are approximately 20 metres of water over structure. The rig is 'cast', as much as it is possible to cast, just in front of the boat and then as the boat drifts over, more line is paid out behind the drift. It is important to maintain a connection with the fly and to keep tension as the line will sink faster than the fly and if gone unchecked will wrap itself around the line. Once the flyline is paid out then the retrieve begins.

There are several retrieves that work. The first is the '**Roly Poly Strip**' much favoured by striped bass fishermen. The rod butt is tucked under the arm and the line is retrieved hand over hand creating a fast and continuous fly motion. The second is the '**Sick Fish Strip**'. Again the rod is tucked under the arm and the line is grabbed by the free hand and then yanked in an upward direction by the other hand. The pace is varied and random giving the fly the motion of a wounded baitfish. Lastly there is the '**Speed Strip**'. The rod is held in the casting hand and the other hand reaches forward as far as possible, pulling the line backwards while simultaneously pushing the rod forwards at the same time. With the speed strip, start slow and then speed up to as fast as you can. This imitates a fleeing baitfish, so picture in your mind's eye Nemo being chased by a massive GT and then swimming for his life. You get the idea. The take, when it comes, is truly savage and can cut into your fingers, so gloves are advisable. Then it just a question of hanging on for dear life, putting a foot on the gunwale and fighting with everything you have got. Apart from GTs, this method also produces black trevally from the depths, numerous reef species and the infamous dog-toothed tuna.

CHAPTER 14 - OTHER TREVALLY SPECIES

BLUEFIN TREVALLY *(Caranx melampygus)* after the giant trevally are perhaps one of the most common fish targeted by fly anglers. Although they do not normally grow as large as their cousins, they are very sought-after due to their magnificent colouring of speckled electric blue. Bluefins normally hunt in packs and are often found in the same areas as GTs. They love the surf line and reef edge where they themselves are safe from predators. The largest recorded specimen is 117cm, but most are between 3-8lb with a real specimen being over 10lb. They move incredibly fast and are extremely aggressive. They will attack flies nearly the same size as them, often not being able to get their mouth around the hook. If you wish to target bluefin trevally specifically, then go down fly and leader size and strip as fast as you can or they veer off and lose interest. Many believe that pound for pound they fight harder than GTs themselves. Bluefin trevally are particularly partial to crustaceans and, like GTs, they use their colour to blend in with surroundings. On the flats they are particularly fond of areas that combine sand and coral.

BLUEFIN

GOLDEN

BLACK

GOLDEN TREVALLY (*Gnathanodon speciosus*) are very different to their brethren in that they have proboscis they can extend to suck up cephalopods, molluscs and crustaceans. They are the trevally equivalent to permit and feed on similar creatures. They prefer clear water and can be found tailing on the flats. However, unlike permit they have that aggressive trevally nature and they chase their prey down. To catch one on the fly is an achievement. They tend to be found on turtle grass flats, sand and marl flats along with blue holes contained in the flats. Once hooked, this species is extremely powerful and will test your tackle. They normally school together and are actually quite easily caught, dredging in deep water. Unlike GTs they are not normally boat-shy and the largest specimen I have heard of was 26lb, landed on Farquhar in the Seychelles.

BLACK TREVALLY (*Caranx lugubris*) are a deep water trevally found along the reef edge or deep on structure. They are often found in water over 30 meters in depth where black is a good colour to hunt. They are normally only caught when flyfishermen are dredging but in that environment are another great gamefish. Characterised by their dark black colouring, black scutes along the flank and abnormally large dorsal fin, their mouth is considerably more pouty than some of the other species. They are known to feed on fish, crustaceans and molluscs on reef edges and drop-offs. Black trevally are normally solitary fish but sometimes move in small schools and interestingly enough not always with their own species. They are often seen following oceanic white tip sharks in deeper water. When hooked they are very strong like most Carangidae and in deeper water present their own challenges to land as they will battle you with everything they have.

BLUDGER

YELLOW SPOT

BLUDGER TREVALLY (*Carangoides gymnostethus*) like slightly shallower water than black trevally - approximately 12 meters in depth. They generally gravitate around coral reefs, rock pinnacles and offshore structures. They are more torpedo-shaped than a yellowspot trevally but less heavily marked. This species are generally silvery green in colour with green tipped fins and, exhibiting a more rubbery mouth, they slightly resemble a small amber jack and will travel in large schools. They have no teeth but a strong jaw the texture of sand paper which suggests they are particularly fond of molluscs such as tropical squid. Generally caught through dredging, they are extremely powerful and their barrel-like shape is solid muscle. They are most commonly found off the east coast of Africa, across the Indian Ocean, and have become highly-prized in Mozambique where they are targeted specifically as a gamefish.

YELLOW SPOT TREVALLY (*Carangoides fulvoguttatus*) are occasionally found in the flats and although they don't normally grow very large, they can provide some great sport on light tackle. They normally live in lagoon systems or in deeper water in schools and eat very similar things to bonefish and golden trevally such as prawns, mantis shrimp and small fish species. These little muggers don't normally appear very often but when they do, they give you a huge surprise when fishing on the flats as the 'bonefish' you thought you had hooked starts peeling off line and is unwilling to turn.

BRASSY

BRASSY TREVALLY (*Caranx papuensis*, also known as the Brassy kingfish, Papuan trevally, Tea-leaf trevally and Green back trevally) is another generally smaller trevally species that you occasionally bump into on the flats. Found right across the Indian Ocean and as far south as Australia, these broad-nosed fish are often mistaken as small GTs because like their large cousins they remain quite silver when juvenile with black spotting toward the tail. They only develop their distinctive brassy hue by the time they mature and become larger.

A specimen bluefin trevally
from the Nubian flats in Sudan

PART II

DESTINATIONS

There are many areas around the globe that are home to giant trevally and the following section highlights the areas currently deemed as the worlds hotspots.

Each chapter has been crafted by those who know these areas intimately and are either long-standing guides, operators or pioneers who discovered them. Their stories will enlighten and captivate you.

CHAPTER 15 - ALPHONSE ISLAND, SEYCHELLES SERGE SAMSON

St Francois Atoll

Seven degrees south of the equator, 310 nautical miles south-west of Mahé and deep into Seychellois waters, lies one of the Indian Ocean's best-known atolls: Alphonse.

Usually included as part of the Amirantes chain, Alphonse is approximately 87 miles south of the main Amirantes bank so is more realistically referred to as the Alphonse Group. This consists of three coralline atolls: Alphonse, Bijoutier and St Francois. Appearing on Portuguese charts collectively as 'San Francisco' until 1730, Chevalier Alphonse de Pontevez, commanding French frigate *Le Lys*, visited the islands and gave what is now an arrow-shaped island, bisected by a runway, his name: Alphonse. San Francisco became St Francois and the third, much smaller atoll lying between Alphonse and St Francois, became Bijoutier, the 'jewel'.

Alphonse has changed hands many times since being bought in 1823 by the Huteau family and disputes over the ownership of the island meant that Alphonse only became part of the

Serge Samson at the
tiller of 'GT Dream'

Seychelles in 1881. There was sufficient food and water to sustain a small population and the fertile deposits of guano gave rise to a productive copra plantation. Between 1925 and 1955 over a million coconuts were harvested annually and exported along with turtle meat and shells. The world turned, times moved on, commodity markets changed and by the mid 1990s Alphonse was attracting attention of a very different nature.

Explorers once more ventured south, this time armed with fly rods and using live-aboard yachts to access these remote atolls. *Tam Tam*, owned and run at the time by Martin and Anna Lewis, ventured south of Mahé with a cargo of flyfishermen to explore the waters of Alphonse and St Francois. She eventually made her home on Alphonse and was an iconic part of the development and growth of Alphonse as a flyfishing destination. She 'retired', making her last journey between Alphonse and Mahé in 2012. The lodge was opened in 1999 on the island and the fishing was managed by two companies who split the 12 rods granted by the government between them.

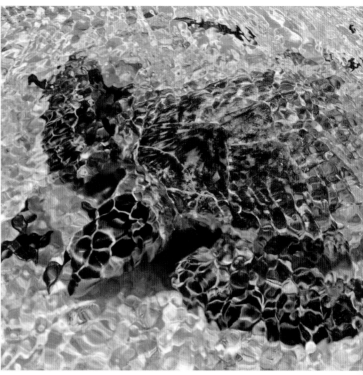

It wasn't always a harmonious existence but in-keeping with the island's previous history, the management of the island has continued to change hands passing from the original two companies to Shackleton International who in turn were replaced by Great Plains Seychelles and on to the current custodians of the atolls, Alphonse Island Fishing Company.

Alphonse covers a relatively small 8km² area including the reef, flats and the lagoon. A deep but narrow channel, the 'Canal de la Mort', separates Alphonse from the reef that protects tiny Bijoutier and beyond that lies the St Francois lagoon. While Alphonse gets the credit and is the name most associated with one of the most prolific and varied saltwater flyfishing destinations in the world, it is the horse-shoe shaped St Francois that is the real treasure. With a relatively small land mass, the total area of St Francois including reef, flats and lagoon covers an area in excess of 40km². Within that not-inconsiderable area lies the lagoon itself, a calm and peaceful oasis surrounded by the tumult of the reef itself. Hard white sand flats, small pancake flats, finger flats and a few areas of turtle grass provide a unique environment for anglers to wade, eyes searching for the distinctive shape of a GT cruising the flats. For the adventurous, a walk to the edge will invariably produce results as GTs hunt the surf line. For those inside the reef, the channels are thoroughfares for hunter and hunted alike as the tidal push draws prey species onto and off the flats. The environments are diverse, the species count high; it is a fully-laden GT buffet atoll.

A FIRST ALPHONSE GT

Looking back over the many years I have spent guiding on Alphonse I remember one particular time that stands out. I took a guy called Ian on his first fishing trip on Alphonse and he was obsessed about GTs. He has been fishing some other outer islands of the Seychelles before, such as Farquhar, Cosmoledo and a few others. That particular day was tough and I searched many places inside the lagoon. We searched everywhere but were unlucky, with many of my usual spots being empty of GTs. At lunchtime I took him to my favourite place, 'Tam Tam channel' as it was low tide and I know that this is the favourite time for GTs. They use this channel for travelling in and out from the flats and it's a good place to stake out. We had lunch and watched the channel as the tide began to push, I hoped bringing the GTs in after food. We stayed there for about two hours as the water looked very clean and perfect fish conditions and I was very hopeful.

Ian made a few small blind casts into the blue of the channel amongst the coral bommies but sadly nothing happened. Finally we were about to move to another place but almost as soon as I pulled up the anchor I saw two big white GTs going out of the channel and I began to get very excited. I quickly asked him to go in the front of my skiff and to make a long cast. He was very fast and made that cast with the fly landing very near the fish, good cast! The two big GTs turned and followed his fly slowly. He was very excited and from where I was standing on top of the poling platform I could see his legs were shaking. He started to strip the fly very fast – too fast – and the line got shorter and shorter, only about 15ft to the skiff. I said 'Slow down man! Slow down! Stop!' The GT slowly followed. I had to tell him to slowly start to strip again. I just saw the big mouth of the GT open and swallow the fly. The other one was alongside and was bigger but after a few seconds, he spooked.

As soon as the GT turned I shouted to Ian to set the hook! The GT turned and dived deep up the channel towards the lagoon in a long hard run with Ian's rod bouncing as he tried to control the line. He stripped so much line onto the deck, a big tangle jumped up and smashed into

Tam Tam Channel, St Francois

the bottom ring, pulling the top three sections of his rod into the water. The line and rod shot off into the channel after the GT with Ian holding onto the handle and the reel. I had to quickly start the engine and follow the GT as there were many coral heads around and I needed him to keep his line very short to stop him getting cut. He wound the line in and I ran down and grabbed the rod in the water, undid the tangle, and put the rod together again. As Ian tried to hold the fish high, the GT kept following the

channel and ran through the corals and I had to carefully drive around the corals, making the same move as the GT. At that point I started to get worried that the GT would try to swim to the *Tam Tam* buoy rope, as Ian would have lost it.

After about 35 minutes of hard fighting from Ian, the GT was finally getting tired. I moved the skiff over to the nearest finger flat and we both carefully got off and onto the solid ground. The fish was still pulling, but he came up onto his side and I knew he was nearly beaten. I spoke to Ian encouragement and finally he could drag the fish near and I got my hands round the tail and we landed him! He was a big fish, maybe 80lb. To that day it was his biggest battle and his biggest GT in his fishing career and we were both laughing. Ian still keeps the picture on his phone as it is his biggest memory on Alphonse and his GT dream. Since that day he returned to Alphonse many times and we have been catching lots of GTs together. I still tell him the other one was bigger…

CHAPTER 16 - ASTOVE ATOLL, SEYCHELLES WAYNE HASELAU

Astove Atoll lies 104km south-west of Mahé and forms part of the south-eastern-most island group in the Seychelles – the Aldabra group. Astove shares the same volcanic base as Cosmoledo and rises 4km from the ocean floor. It is a continuous landmass of 661 hectares and measures 5km north-to-south, 3km east-to-west and circles a lagoon of approximately 5km². The single channel entrance is called Gueule Bas Channel and is 100 metres at its widest. The Aldabra group consists of four islands including Aldabra, Astove, Assumption and Cosmoledo. Each of the islands is unique. Plans are underway to develop the eco-tourism potential here, especially for scuba diving and catch-and-release flyfishing. Aldabra is famous as it is a designated world heritage site and is the second largest raised atoll in the world. Astove, although much smaller than Aldabra, is its geological twin and is also a raised atoll encircling a central, ecologically unique lagoon which is a visual splendour.

Peter Moylan & Wayne Haselau

Astove is dominated by a magnificent, extensive central tidal lagoon which fills and drains through a single narrow shallow channel in the south-western corner of the island. The marine eco-system in this lagoon is very delicately balanced and dependant on the tidal water ingress and egress from the sea during the various moon phases. The lagoon is very shallow and is extremely nutrient-rich with the seabed consisting of soft, fine white clay-like mud, for the most part. Windy conditions lead to the bottom sediments stirring up and fairly rapidly the water becomes chalky. As a consequence the water in the lagoon is often milky which aids in concealing juvenile fish from predators. Due to its shallowness, the lagoon water also heats up rapidly in sunny conditions. Closer to the mouth, the bottom is soft white sand, suitable for wading. The shallowness of the lagoon makes it a very good habitat for crustaceans and an excellent nursery for juvenile fish. Large numbers of juvenile trevally, bonefish and milkfish are present and this could be the single most important nursery for milkfish in the western Indian Ocean. The lagoon is also an important feeding area for both Hawksbill and Green turtles.

The outside of the atoll is surrounded by deep water and on the western side it has a sheer wall which drops away for several hundred meters. The diving is fabulous with incredibly clear water, with many large fish species, turtles and cetaceans prevalent. The wall is honey-combed by caves and fissures. It was filmed during the Cousteau expedition in the 1970s and is famous in scuba diving lore. The episode featuring Astove is named simply *The Wall*.

The fringing reefs are fairly narrow around the atoll and rise above the surf line to steep sandy or rocky beaches. These beaches are home to large numbers of green turtles which feed and nest on the atoll. It is one of the largest nesting sites for green turtles in the Indian Ocean. The adults are very large and it is not unusual for 60 or more adult turtles to haul themselves out per night in peak nesting season. The competition for space is critical and it is fairly common for turtles to dig up existing nests to lay their eggs. Astove is a very hot island and is as a consequence a superb incubation site for turtles. When the juvenile turtles hatch in late summer they are prey for many species of bird, fish and crustaceans. GTs love to eat juvenile turtles and actively hunt them along the beaches at this time. As a consequence, large numbers of GTs over a metre are to be found patrolling turtle-nesting beaches in the late summer.

The shoreline in the west consists of a steep sandy beachhead at high tide, dropping down to narrow 200m-wide coral and marl flats, covered in mixed eelgrass and turtlegrass populated by large bonefish, triggerfish and bluefin trevally. GTs are common on these flats but are forced off to the edge of the reef on the extreme low spring tide, which drops by over three metres. The rise is rapid and the fishing here is fast and furious on the pushing spring tide. The western side of the island is in the lee for the dominant south-eastern monsoon. The eastern side of the island is comprised of shelving rock formations of ancient layers of sedimentary rock formed from coral debris. Large slabs of this rock have broken away and have accumulated in many areas at the top of the beach crest, creating a completely differed type of shoreline. This is the wild or windward side for most of the year and is covered in all kinds of natural and man-made marine debris such as buoys, FADs, large hardwood logs and evidence of a number of wrecks. The fringing reef here is narrow in the north-east, between 50-100 metres, widening out in the south east to 250m.

There are a number of bays and longitudinal crevices in the rock running out from the shore on this side of the island. Triggerfish, bonefish and bluefin trevally are prolific here as well as large numbers of rudderfish, surgeons and snappers. Shoals of mullet are also to be found. As with the west, the turn of the tide and the first part of the pushing tide is best for GTs in the surf. The difference here on the rocky shore of the wild side is the many large rock crabs which are to be found. They seem to be in a constant and deadly dance with the ever-present moray eels which hunt them ruthlessly. These two species are hunted in turn by the GTs who seem to delight in pursuing them at high tide, right in close to shore and amongst the rocks. The high tide forces a

The perfect day

lot of potential prey such as mullet and rudderfish right into the white water of the shore break so that this area becomes a veritable smörgåsbord for the GTs. Throw some hatchling turtles into the mix and you get the idea.

The Astove lagoon mouth is possibly one of, if not the most, prime GT spots on the planet due to its location. Large numbers of fish move in and out of the lagoon daily and they must do so through this narrow channel. It is like a prime river beat on a top salmon river, because the fish are to be found in moving water. The tempting prospect of the huge numbers of baitfish in the lagoon draws GTs to the area. Due to its small acreage, it is sensitive to fishing pressure and will have to be very carefully managed in order to remain productive. There are some mangroves in the lagoon which enhance the productivity of the area considerably. These mangroves are prime hunting areas for GTs, as large numbers of baitfish and crustaceans shelter amongst the swamps, especially at high tide.

The tides affect the fishing on Astove and spring tides are definitely best for GTs, especially in the surf. However, the window of opportunity is brief, as a great deal of water is moving on these tides. Fishing the surf on the last part of the drop and first part of the push is extremely productive, as is the high tide when the fish are close in to the shore, especially on the wild side. Fishing in the lagoon is also best on spring tides. Neap tides are productive on Astove although the fish are more spread out, as there is water on the flats for longer periods of time. The neap tide push is slower and allows more time to walk on the seaward flats. A limited amount of offshore teasing for GTs is possible on Astove and broadens the windows of opportunity, but it does affect the fishing in the long-term as experienced on Alphonse. It is also possible to dredge for GTs here and, while this is not ideal, as the flats are so good, it is a good way to take a trophy fish when all else fails.

THE HAIDER INCIDENT – ASTOVE AT ITS BEST

In December 2012 I had the privilege to fish and guide for the first time on Astove. I had always wanted to fish this fabled atoll, so finally to be there and guide was a real treat. Astove has a reputation for large GTs, most of which are taken in the surf or on the reef flats. To fish Astove effectively, one has to be prepared to walk, as the fish move around and need to be located. There are a few particularly choice areas: the channel mouth between sea and lagoon; the reef between the island and the North Point and the wreck beat on the south-east of the island. In March 2013 I found myself on the beach at the then-deserted settlement sitting in the shade under the large Casurina trees having lunch with my two guests for the day, Alex and Stephan Haider. The fishing had been tough on Cosmoledo due to poor weather conditions the previous couple of days, so the pressure was on to get them into big fish while the weather held.

We started the day walking through to the inner lagoon and experienced some sublime bonefishing on the flats in the upper lagoon. It was a high neap tide and there were tailing bones as far as the eye could see in the ankle-deep water. It was an absolute blast and Alex and Stephan were shouting and whooping as they nailed double after double. After a couple of hours I suggested we walk back to look for GTs along the beach. On a previous trip I had encountered some really large GTs cruising along there on a high tide and I wanted to see if I could put my guests into one. We staked out in the shade and had lunch, all the while looking for fish. Stephan was amping and so I had a quick sandwich before heading out with him along the beach towards

the north point. Alex said he wanted to hang back and take his time taking photographs and fishing for smaller quarry along the beach. Large GTs patrol this section of beach feeding on bonefish, mullet and small trevally. Occasionally, a turtle nest will hatch during daylight which these big fish know. They are always on the lookout for these hatchlings which is one of their favourite prey.

I had encountered some of these large turtle-eaters here previously, so I was prepared when a large single fish came cruising down the edge of the beach in less than a metre of crystal-clear blue water. It is a majestic and awe-inspiring sight to see one of these big hungry dragons cruising confidently, looking for prey. To see a large GT lit up and hunting in shallow water is one of the greatest moments in flats flyfishing and it takes a lot to keep your composure. I pointed at the fish giving Stephan the heads-up while it was still more than 50 metres away, calling the distance and giving him last-minute instructions and encouragement.

As it rapidly came within range I waited breathlessly while the whole saga unfolded, Stephan making a superb cast slightly to the side and in front. The fish lit up, locking onto the 6/0 brush fly, big pectoral wings set as it came up on step and engulfed the fly, its massive head half out of the water. Stephan struck hard as the beast surged away for the reef and deep water. A real

battle royale was developing as Stephan put on the brakes, applying maximum pressure to prevent the big fish from making the coral reef and cutting us off. Suddenly I noticed there was another large GT shadowing the hooked fish in sympathy and excitement. By now Stephan had his approximately 40kg fish close to the beach and I was desperately trying to guide Alex into a double. Casting at a free-swimming trevally which is shadowing another hooked fish is usually a sure-fire way of getting another hook-up. While it may sometimes seem like cheating, in such a situation it is the hot ticket.

By now Alex had read the situation and was casting close to the hooked fish in an effort to hook-up. A good cast, the fly lands, one strip and *Bam!* the other fish nails it!! *Double!!* All the while, I am shouting instructions and taking photos as the fresh fish makes a long run. I put my kevlar tailing glove on and attempted to get close to Stephan's monster. As I stepped off the edge of the beach into deeper water, I raised my eyes and to my disbelief a shoal of eight or more GTs of a similar size bore down on me. Before I can get onto land I was literally attacked by these fish who were now pumped up with excitement. Their infamous shoal aggression had kicked into top gear and they were having a go at my legs! Mayhem ensued as I was bitten a couple of times while I tried to kick them away, all the while trying to get my hand around the caudal stem of Stephan's big fish. At last I had a good hold; all the while Alex was playing his fish like a pro. I handed Stephan's fish over to him and went to tail Alex's fish. Dodging the ever-present shoal I managed to tail his fish as well and we had effectively achieved the impossible. Two trophy fish in 20 minutes – we were shouting, screaming, hand-shaking and back slapping. I was absolutely thrilled! Big smiles and big fish – unbelievable... Such is GT fishing on fly, the ultimate adrenalin-rush. Astove does it again!

CHAPTER 17 - THE CORAL SEA & GREAT BARRIER REEF, AUSTRALIA

DAMON OLSEN

The Coral Sea and the remote Far Northern Great Barrier Reef are amongst the most remote and difficult to access coral feefs in the world. The Great Barrier Reef is also the world's largest living organism, and is over 2½ times larger than any other Coral Reef system on Earth, stretching over 2,600km along the Australian coastline and covering more than 300,000 square kilometres. It is fair to say that because of the size and biodiversity of the reef structure it produces some of the most consistently prolific sportfishing in the world. There can be many reasons for this, but the primary reason is that there is a very small amount of fishing pressure spread over a very large area. This offers anglers the ability to fish areas that are rarely, if ever, fished by other anglers, and the subsequent results are as you would expect of a frontier and untouched location.

There are a few facts to highlight about the Great Barrier Reef and associated Coral Sea. The total reef area of the Great Barrier Reef is larger than the combined reef area of Papua New Guinea, Fiji, Vanuatu, The Solomon Islands, Micronesia, The Cook Islands, The Hawaiian Islands and

Peter Morse with an Aussie GT

New Caledonia combined. The coral reef is what supports the fish life, so more reef equals more fish. Some 15% of all fish species known to live on earth can be found in the Great Barrier Reef, yet it covers less that 0.01% of the earth's ocean surface. The Great Barrier Reef is recognised as having the largest biodiversity of coral reef fish species on earth; it is the world's largest Coral Reef system; and the spawning aggregations of big GTs and 1000lb+ black marlin have not been observed anywhere else on earth. Finally it is the most protected and healthiest reef system on earth, with over 30% designated as no fishing at all.

What is the difference between the Coral Sea and the Great Barrier Reef? The Coral Sea is part of the Pacific Ocean, and is the name of the part of the Pacific that borders the northeast Australian coastline and extends east to Vanuatu and north to Papua New Guinea. The Great Barrier Reef is the line of fringing reef that extends all the way up the Australian coast, but further out to sea from this reef edge lies a set of reefs known as the Coral Sea Island Territories, which are part of

Australian waters, and stretch over 400 nautical miles seaward. The outer Coral Sea Reefs such as Kenn, Wreck, Marion, Cato, Frederick, Willis Islets and Diamond Islets are small and isolated coral-fringed reefs that few people have ever visited, but they were the setting for the first trips ever conducted on Nomad Sportfishing's mothership *Odyssey II* in 2005.

The Nomad Sportfishing Charter operation started at Fraser Island on the Queensland coast, and first made news with the catch and release of a GT that measured 1.64m long from lower jaw to tail fork. This fish was estimated at over 80kg, and is still one of the largest GTs ever landed. The lure of fishing the remote Coral Sea Island Territories was always on the horizon, ever since Nomad Sportfishing was established, but it was not until the construction of a purpose-built mothership, complete with jet fuel storage and refuelling capabilities that this became a reality in August 2005. The first trips to Kenn and Wreck Reef were conducted using a seaplane to fly the 300 nm distance to sea, transporting excited anglers from the mainland. The first anglers to ever fly into Kenn Reef by seaplane landed to experience fishing that was truly once-in-a-lifetime stuff.

Odyssey II

Over subsequent years Nomad Sportfishing explored most of the Coral Sea Island Territories, including Kenn, Wreck, Cato, Frederick, Marion, Flinders Reefs and also the Diamond Islets. The fishing around these remote atolls was at times simply superb, and produced some of the most intense sportfishing action for GTs, dogtooth tuna, yellowfin tuna and wahoo that anyone had ever seen. Some trips produced unheard-of numbers of GTs of epic proportions, including the first-ever trip to Kenn reef which resulted in over 300 GTs landed in five days, but with 50 of those GTs weighing over 40kg; 20 of them over 50kg; and five over 60kg. This was the GT fishing that dreams were made of.

However after a few seasons of fishing exclusively in the remote outer Coral Sea, the operation started to focus some of its time on the outer edge of some of the more remote parts of the Great Barrier Reef with great success, and yet more prolific GT fishing. Part of the reason for this change in focus was the unpredictable nature of the GT fishing on the remote and isolated outer Coral Sea reefs. It was found that the GT fishing with any kind of surface lure was completely reliant on baitfish called sauris being present in the shallow reef edges and lagoons. These baitfish would only hold in the shallows when the ocean current was coming from a particular direction, and with enough speed to cause upwellings into the reef shallows. When these conditions occurred, the GT fishing was simply incredible, with monster 50kg+ GTs literally on tap for those who could stop them in the shallow water. However the ocean current is not linked to moon phase or tides, but is controlled by complex ocean currents, winds and forces which cannot be predicted. This lack of predictability makes it difficult to schedule trips with anglers coming from all over the world, so the focus for GT fishing switched to the outer Great Barrier Reef. With a labyrinth of reef to explore, the learning continues to this day, as do the prolific reports of GT catches beyond imagination. The most recent report from *Odyssey II* [2016] was of one of the Nomad boats with three anglers on the far northern Great Barrier Reef releasing over 100 GTs in a day between 25-45kg in size.

Currently the operation uses an 80ft mothership called *Odyssey II* as the floating hotel and fuel reserve to service the 3-4 guided sportfishing vessels that take anglers fishing each day. The 18-25ft sportfishing vessels return to the mothership, anchored in a calm and protected reef anchorage each night and then begin fishing again each morning. The use of a mothership means you can explore the full length of the Great Barrier Reef and Coral Sea, and only fish each area for 1-3 weeks each year. These trips to these remote areas vary from 3-6 days aboard the mothership, with the longer trips accessing the more remote areas. The vessel is positioned at different locations along the remote northeast coast throughout the year and small charter flights take anglers to meet up with the mothership at the various locations.

THE EXTRAORDINARY MARION REEF

One of the most memorable experiences from my many years fishing the Coral Sea & Great Barrier Reef involves a period of time at Marion Reef when the current was just right, and for an entire four week spell we were anchored at this reef with guests flying in and out each week via seaplane. We were seeing, but not catching, some of the biggest GTs I have ever laid eyes on. We first encountered these monster fish one day when idling along the reef edge and seeing a huge

Coral heads of Marion Reef

commotion on the surface up ahead. I pointed this out to Malcolm and Chris who were with me at the time. It appeared to be two large sharks on top of a shallow one metre-deep bommie, fighting over what appeared to be a substantial coral trout in the 10-12kg range. We idled closer to the commotion to get a look at what we thought were sharks and could hardly believe our eyes as it dawned on all of us at once that this fight was lasting too long for it to be sharks. The shapes we could see fighting over the coral trout were not sharks, but a pair of monstrous GTs fighting over this coral trout, both trying to eat it. As you can imagine, poppers rained down on top of these huge fish, but with their focus on 10-12kg of coral trout, they were not interested in our rather pathetic-looking poppers.

We all simply watched as the events unfolded over the next 30 seconds. The massive GTs broke this fish apart and then calmly swam off the edge of the bommie and disappeared into the clear sandy bottom. Now these fish were both over 7ft long and were of a proportion that I have never seen before or since. Keeping in mind that we've landed several GTs over 1½m long, these things were in another class and size entirely. I cannot really begin to estimate their size, but somewhere well over 100kg would be conservative. After the realisation that there were some monster GTs in this area, and after we had all calmed down and discussed what we had just seen, it was time to get into some fishing in this area where these giants had been seen. What we then found and experienced in this area of reef over the following weeks was regular encounters with some GTs of truly mind-blowing proportions.

The area we had found was a shallow coral lagoon on the outside edge of the reef, and at low tide some of the areas of reef were exposed, but between these exposed bommies ran channels and crevices in the reef that were 2-4 metres deep. What we found was that the massive GTs would sit in these channels and crevices and wait for the rising tide to wash food and baitfish over the top of the reef and they would then pounce on the unsuspecting reef fish. These GTs were actually targeting things like snapper, groupers and emperors on the reef shallows; their preference seemed to be for 3-5kg fish to eat. Whilst drifting over the shallow reef flats you would often see explosions on the surface where it looked like barrels had been dropped from a great height, but it was just the resident GTs demolishing large reef fish for afternoon tea!

The big issue in this terrain was landing the fish. Each day for about two hours when the tide was just right, we would be hooking up two to three of these massive fish, with battles lasting between one second and five minutes, but they all ended in bust-offs in the reef due to the shallow water and skinny channels that the fish were swimming along. The GTs were so aggressive that one fish of 50kg+ that we thought was beaten, and was just under the boat in two metres of water, had the lure smashed out of its mouth when another much larger GT charged at it out of nowhere just as we grabbed the leader. The bigger GT was trying to eat the popper hanging out of the other fish's mouth, and the end result was the popper being dislodged and us ending up with no fish.

We tried everything to land these fish, even spooling a reel up with 40m of 200lb fluorocarbon leader and attempting to tease and switch one of these monster fish, but even that ended in demolition in the reef. These fish were all massive, and looking at them in the water, they all looked like 50-70kg monsters, but the frustration of not being able to extract them was wearing thin. We were landing the odd fish of 30kg in this shallow water, but the majority of fish were massive and we reached a point after a few weeks where it was about 40-0 to the big GTs, and you can imagine we were rather demoralised at this failure to land any of them.

On the last day of the four week trip we did get lucky and landed what we called a 'small one'. Liam was on the rod and myself and Tim Baker were guiding him and we told him it was just a small one and were not even too concerned about driving the boat for him until it screamed off 30m of line under crazy heavy locked drag and we started the chase. This 'small one' was estimated at around 55kg and it honestly looked little in the shallow water compared to the creatures we had seen over previous weeks. At least landing one of them showed us it was possible, but the size and quantity of those fish is something I had never seen before or since. We figured there must have been a spawning aggregation of fish there but seeing that many truly gigantic fish in an area that nobody ever fishes, and pretty much still never fishes, was an absolute privilege and something that nobody on those trips will ever forget.

A beast

CHAPTER 18 - COSMOLEDO ATOLL, SEYCHELLES

KEITH ROSE-INNES

The three trees, Cosmoledo Lagoon

Lying 560 miles south west of Mahé is a large, deserted atoll which is wild and untouched. It forms part of the Aldabra group, one of the three clusters of coralline islands known as the 'Outer Islands'. The atoll's name is Cosmoledo, a stone's throw away from the world heritage site of Aldabra and in many respects it resembles the latter. It is often referred to as the Galapagos of the Indian Ocean and this huge atoll is planet earth's giant trevally headquarters.

Cosmoledo consists of a coral ring about eight miles wide, with four major islands on the cardinal points of the compass. Menai and Wizard Islands occupy the east and west points and were named after the two ships that explored the atoll on the Moresby Expedition in 1822. The south island sits near the main entrance to the inner lagoon, while the second smaller entrance is just south of Menai. The northern islands are interspersed with numerous islets and banks. Cosmoledo is a true example of natural regeneration. This atoll, along with Aldabra, Assumption, Astove, Marie Louise, Desnoeufs and Remire, was one of those rented by the government to produce

Three Amigos

commodities. In the nineteenth century, Cosmoledo produced tobacco, tomatoes, cotton and later copra, maize and gironom (a variety of gourd or pumpkin). Sea turtles were exploited on a large scale, along with hundreds of tons of the famous burgot (a big shellfish whose thick shell is used to make mother-of-pearl buttons). Until the 1970s the copra fields were worked, but when the costs of producing it exceeded its market value, production ceased.

Left to itself for many decades, Cosmoledo is now simply the home to a rejuvenated eco-system. Along with the abundance of all sea life which frequents this atoll is a legion of giants. Firstly, there is the lazy giant tortoise, some over a hundred years old, lounging in the shade of the palms. Then, in the shallows as far as the eye can see, giant sea turtles prepare to mate. But, more importantly – and the reason why I have made the journey countless times – the waters surrounding Cosmoledo are the domain of huge GTs. So much so that Cosmoledo has become known as the best GT fishery in the world. There is nowhere on this planet where so many GTs come onto the shallow flats to feed.

Cosmoledo is a wild, remote and desolate place steeped in myth and history. When I think back to the 315 days I spent at Cosmoledo in the early years, it is best described as being caught up in a modern version of the ancient great exploration stories. The GT was the treasure, a bounty left for others to find. There were shipwrecks, pirates and in the end some amazing memories and lessons.

In order to do these trips you needed a self-sufficient vessel that can venture 1030km from Mahé and stay in this remote area for a lengthy period. A guest's visit to this Indian Ocean Shangri-La begins with a three-hour charter flight from Mahé to Assumption, Cosmoledo's closest island with an operational airstrip. Cosmoledo is an eight hour sail from Assumption so the ship has to be well stocked and equipped, as there is no coming back until the end of the trip.

My first trips to Cosmoledo were on board the *Mieke*, a 110ft Grand Bank schooner, which was sailed all the way up to the Seychelles from Port Elizabeth, South Africa. During the exploration of the inside of the lagoon, the Captain quickly realised that the charts were inaccurate as on two occasions her large steel hull was left stranded high and dry. Strangely in 2004 whilst on her way back to the Seychelles and in flat calm seas, she sank off Mozambique into over a thousand metres of water. To quickly fill the void we then chartered the *Indian Ocean Explorer*, a 100ft exploration vessel used in the past by Jacques Cousteau. In 2007 she ended up on the reef at Alphonse Island and once floated and refitted, was taken by pirates in 2009. After long negotiations which lasted 89 days, the crew were released and the pirates sank her off the Somalian coast, and thus came the closure of the outer waters to any vessels.

It's been a long hard journey back, with the Seychelles finally ridding their waters of pirates by late 2013. Unmanned drones and now radar stations ensure the waters are safe and trips to this magnificent atoll recommenced in March 2014. The *Mayas Dugong* is now the platform used. She is an ex-research vessel, which has been upgraded and modified into a mother ship catering for long-range flyfishing expeditions. As a flyfisherman it would be difficult to find a better boat from which to operate, with its ability to store and transport four tender boats on its spacious aft deck.

THE EARLY DAYS

I can recall my first visit to Cosmoledo and first fishing session as if it were yesterday. That first morning a fiery sunrise mirrored on the glassy water of the southern entrance of the lagoon, welcoming us to the atoll. If seen at high tide, the lack of flats might make you think you were in the wrong place, but as the tide quickly drops, you realise how much water you have to cover. This southern entrance, sometimes referred to as a roaring river, makes you quickly understand how large the tidal rise and fall are. The charts show a two-and-a-half metre shift, but the experience would make you think that it is in the region of three to four metres. Seychelles' sand flats are unlike most others in the world. The sand is white and hard, making wading easy.

After a short boat ride, like a sniper onto a battlefield, I jump off into the water. At nine o'clock, two 30lb-range GTs appear. With my rod firmly locked under my arm, I strip off as much line as possible and tighten the drag. With the thought 'make them chase something' firmly ingrained into my subconscious, I made a cast and lead the fish by a couple of metres. As the fly landed there was instant interest. I saw their pectorals extend as they turned. I stripped as fast as possible, the fish followed, jostling for the fly. They created a submarine-like bow wave in the transparent water. Then, with big, black dilated eyes firmly locked on the fly, one fish took the lead. The eyes came straight towards me, then, at exactly the right moment, I missed a strip… Instantaneously, the GT's mouth opened to engulf the fly. With three short, sharp movements I drove the hook home. In a split second the line cleared through my fingers and onto the reel. In a bid for freedom the fish charged for deeper water and as I followed, it dawned on me that this was definitely the highest number of GTs I had seen on any flat. With the tidal flood came waves of GTs, sometimes more than twenty-strong in a group. The action was continuous until the tide had pushed in so high that it was around my waist. I lost count, but during the four days spent at Cosmoledo I caught and released more than 50 GTs.

Since that first experience each group would have at least one similar fishing session to the one I experienced. There would be an amazing incident or sighting each week that was extraordinary and probably something that would only be experienced at Cosmoledo. GTs on average are smaller at Cosmoledo than at Astove Atoll, possibly due to the amount of fish competing for food. There were however some fish that if you called them a monster it would be an understatement. They were so large that quite often we would confuse GTs for sharks. They had so much attitude that a fellow guide Paul Boyers had his feet taken from underneath him by a GT that bit the back of his boot while he was running to land another big GT. This absence of humans for such a long period of time simply meant that these fish were uneducated and totally unfazed about humans. They were living and feeding on the flats as apex predators should and always have before we came along.

Many of the really big GT sightings were from a distance until I had a close encounter with one of the biggest fish I have ever seen. It was a late afternoon pushing spring tide at the south-western channel. The water had been baking on the turtle grass-covered flats, making the water peaty and almost impossible to walk in as it was so hot. The stained hot water had become trapped by the fresh clear water that was pushing in from the ocean side. I had just summoned the skiff when I noticed numerous GTs that were head and tailing in the extremely hot water that had now moved into the channel. We jumped into the boat and moved over to the area where these fish were feeding. Looking into the sun, my three clients cast their flies which were instantaneously attacked by numerous GTs in the 15-20lb range. The action was fast and furious which meant that it was a tug of war to get the fish to the boat as quickly as possible, unhook and release them.

When attempting to release the third fish that I tailed, an enormous mouth appeared and almost completely engulfed the 15lb GT. I let out a bit of a yelp as I battled to get the GT from its mouth while holding the prey by its tail. This was no shark or even a big barracuda, but an enormous GT, with a mouth big enough to fit two of my heads inside. After a couple seconds the mammoth fish released its grip and I was left with a dead mangled GT. Cosmoledo gives you the rare opportunity and privilege of gazing into a world that has changed very little in centuries.

CHAPTER 19 - DESROCHES - SAINT JOSEPH - POIVRE, SEYCHELLES

MATTHIEU COSSON

Desroches Island

Desroches is the closest 'Outer Island' from Mahé as well as the largest of the Amirantes group with 394 hectares of landmass. It was named in honour of François-Julien Desroches, the administrator of Ile de France (Mauritius) in the late-18th century. The hotel opened its doors in 1987 for the first time and since 2009 a handful of 5 star villas facing the beautiful beach have been built. The flyfishing on Desroches flats is difficult as it has no consistency. One day you can spot a school of bonefish and the next day they will be gone. No specific patterns prevail. Somehow during the southeast monsoon, it is possible to find more trevally (yellow spotted, golden, bluefin and GT) on the eastern side of the island.

Poivre Atoll covers 1,467 hectares of reef flats and comprises three islands: Poivre, Florentin and Ile du Sud. It was named after Pierre Poivre, governor of Ile de France and Bourbon (Mauritius and Reunion) in 1771. Saint Joseph is the largest of the three islands with 2,253 hectares of which

nearly 80% are flats. It comprises 14 islands with a lagoon that has no channel to the open ocean. It is to be noted that Saint Joseph and its neighbouring island d'Arros are the only privately-owned 'Outer Islands'. As of 2012, it has belonged to Chelonia Company Ltd. Their management has been handed over to the 'Save Our Seas Foundation' and soon they will be protected under the Seychelles Nature Conservancy Act, which means they will be considered nature reserves without any activities allowed.

In the past, all these islands have been used to produce coconuts and by-products (copra, oil etc) as well as salted fish and a bit of guano. Nowadays, the only activities are hotel operations at Desroches Island as Poivre Atoll does not have any activity going. There are just five Seychellois, working for the Islands Development Company; they maintain the grass airstrip and the small facilities. On the other hand, Saint Joseph Atoll is completely free of human presence.

As these atolls and islands are the closest to Mahé, they have been fished quite heavily with spinning gear by anglers doing live-aboard trips but also by guests from Desroches, fishing conventional tackle. Add to this a relatively small GT population and you have wiser and spookier GTs which spices up the game!

Saint Joseph holds the largest GT population in comparison to Poivre, with Desroches trailing far behind. It is important to bear in mind that these atolls are not like Farquhar, Providence or Cosmoledo; if you have had two-to-four shots a day when looking specifically for them, that is considered a great GT day. Although the fish are forced to either stay in the lagoon or outside, as it lacks a channel, depending on the tides, anglers have good chances if they give it their best (listen to the guide and good casting ability). Neap tides or spring tides produce fish, but it is necessary to target special spots to locate them.

Of course, fishing the push at low tide during spring tides produces the best opportunities but you may find it necessary to walk quite some distance (4 to 5km) to cover the water. When the neap tides show up, it is a great game to try to find GTs looking for mullet schools or swimming with rays and sharks. It all depends on where the warm water will be; pay attention to the wind direction as well. When the tide is low, focus on the edge of the lagoon and on the pancake flats. Blind casting the latter will produce some big surprises! As Poivre Atoll does not have a lagoon, the best spots to fish are the reef flats. Here the structure is far different from Saint Joseph – it is almost level – which means the tide will rise at the same level all around the atoll.

Choose fishing spots wisely and consider how to walk in order not to get caught in the middle of nowhere at high tide as there will be decent-sized bull sharks around. Targeting neap tides will present longer fishing time due to the atoll's structure. For Saint Joseph, better GT fishing is generally had during these tides than during the spring tides. At the drop, it is possible to spot fish moving out, following some of the depressions and cuts then moving along the reef edge. This will give more shots at the same fish if your casting angle hasn't been good at first sight of the GT.

All in all, Saint Joseph and Poivre atolls are great GT venues for fishermen who have had previous encounters with them and that are now eager to test their technical skills. As an aside it is a great option to fish a couple of days at Poivre for Indo Pacific permit as it holds an incredible population of them. The rest of the days can then be spent hunting for GTs. It is difficult to target them during the same day as they move around at the same time of the tide but require two fully opposite sets of mind.

A TALE OF TWO SONS

It's almost 12.30 and the tide will start pushing soon and here I am walking the Mitzi skiff as the water is too skinny. My guests are sitting at the bow to balance out the flats boat – and his younger son sleeping. There is just about a mile to go … 'How did you put yourself in such pain?' I am asking myself.

Looking back at the start of the week, I remembered his youngest son spotting permit and bones on Poivre on the first day out there. I was blown away by this 6 or 7-year-old kid being able to spot fish much better than 90% of our fishing guests. His father, a former Czech professional road cyclist, was casting like a machine to permit and as soon as his fly landed on the water he would hand the flyrod over to his son for him to get the fish. I had struggled as the boy didn't understand English and his father wasn't translating my indications for the strips and direction. It did not matter, though, as the permit were following the fly all day.

I told him: 'Sir, I really want you to hook yourself one of these things and *land* it, and then we can mess around! Do you know how many times a season we see permit so eager to eat the fly like that?' I was having a tough day... That day we hooked three permit and lost them all, plus a couple of bones at hand. The next day, the scenario was pretty much the same with his older son but again no luck on the permit. On his last day at Poivre, before fishing Saint Joseph, the younger son was on the boat again. Fishing was tougher as warm water had built up during the neap tides. We found some permit, we managed a lot of great shots, until one of them finally ate the fly. This time the lad fought his permit like a king and we landed it! It was great to see his smile and his father so proud of him.

Walking back to the pick-up point to get the boat back to Desroches, the father explained that he came here to give his two sons the opportunity to discover what saltwater fishing was all about. In his own words: 'This trip is not about me, but about my sons.' He confirmed, what I've already felt, that his younger son was the craziest one about fishing. He can't cast yet quickly enough in the salt, but he can see, can strip and understand the body-language of the fish... I told myself I will make sure the son will be proud of his father as his father will be proud of him for the last day. So here I am, walking my skiff to meet the push of the surf in the hope to get some GTs at Saint Joseph. I need that skiff as we are in the middle of a huge spring tide so I will need to cruise the backside of the main island after that.

When we arrived close to the highest spot of the reef I woke up the lad and asked his father to stand on the bow, 12-weight ready to cast. The mullet were pushing some nervous water in the shallow edge of the cut but here on the left three Caspian terns were flying with a purpose in mind when suddenly the water splashed with the mullet jumping around. By the sound of the boils, it must have been GTs blasting them. The terns were now flying low, following the GTs. The son was looking, all eyes wide open while I was in chest-deep water fighting the current and walking the boat into position for his dad to make the cast. I spotted two shadows along the dark turtle grass, moving to the left with the terns right on top of them.

Proud moment

'Cast 18 metres at 2 o'clock!' The 5/0 Black-and-Purple landed on the water and I could see a GT already going for it. First strip and we connected! 'Keep tight, keep tight, keep stripping the line!!' I was shouting. I quickly jumped into the skiff, trimmed down the engine and started it to follow the fish but the father was already applying great pressure on the fish. The GT tried to swim back to the ocean pulling the skiff, which was killing it! At the first chance I jumped into the water to leader the GT and tail it. From the water, I could see the eyes of the son, looking at his father. It was just like he witnessed a miracle. His father was a hero!

After a couple of quick pictures, we decided to put the son in for a workout: to bend that 12-weight with a good-sized lemon shark. We headed to a high spot usually crowded with mullet during high tide with sharks busting them. After a couple of minutes, we managed a solid hook-up on a good one. He handed the rod to his son who fought the shark from the boat for safety. Now it was the father's turn to be proud of his son fighting that shark with all his guts and strength. Eleven minutes later we landed it. A lovely 1.67m female lemon shark. The son was hovering inches above the deck of the boat, riding his magic cloud when we took two good pictures. Then we called it a day.

Frankly, I've landed hundreds of GTs guiding Cosmoledo, Astove, Farquhar and Alphonse but never had a GT made me so happy. These moments are the ones I guide for. To provide happiness to our clients. Guiding is not about you, the guide, or the biggest fish you get compared to the other guides or feeding your ego, it's about understanding your client and making it happen.

CHAPTER 20 - FARQUHAR, SEYCHELLES

JAKO LUCAS

The pets from above, Farquhar Atoll

Farquhar Atoll is the most southerly atoll in the Seychelles chain of islands, lying just over 700km southwest of the main island Mahé. This remote atoll has a total surface area of 170km², including a large lagoon stretching 18km from north to south and 9km from east to west. These main groups of islands form a long curve, largest of which are Isle du Nord and Ile du Sud, with the smaller Manaha gaps and islands between them. Further south is Goulette and to the open western side of the atoll lies the small group known as Trois Îles. The large ear-shaped lagoon provides easy access to the countless flats, channels and surf zones, which make Farquhar such a diverse fishery.

The Farquhar and Aldabra group of islands are unique and unusual as they have been submerged and emerged countless times since their formation – it is estimated that they were submerged about 125,000 years ago. The Farquhar islands are inhospitable coralline, as opposed to the granitic islands further north in Seychelles. Farquhar was discovered in 1501 by Joao da Nova,

Jako Lucas and a Farquhar bus

a Portuguese explorer, and was under British control until 1976, after which it became part of Seychelles at the time of its independence.

Over the past few years, Farquhar has become synonymous with the term 'flyfishing paradise' and has provided all those fortunate enough to visit her shores with the opportunity to fish some of the finest and most productive flats the Indian Ocean has to offer. These flats consist of hard white sand, turtle grass and broken coral, which makes for comfortable wading. Anglers can wade and sight fish to an impressive variety of species that include bonefish, trevally species including the ferocious trophy-sized GT, the finicky Indo-Pacific permit, triggerfish, barracuda, bumphead parrotfish and milkfish. The environment is perfect for stalking bonefish in skinny water, throwing crab flies at the colourful and charismatic tailing triggerfish and holding your nerve as a large GT charges your fly. Added to that, deep water begins very close to shore making it possible to tussle with the monsters that prowl the deep blue.

The stalk

THE BIRD HUNTERS OF FARQUHAR

Having been a guide full time now for nearly a decade, arriving on Farquhar for the first time in 2007, I have been fortunate enough to walk many miles around most of the atolls in the Seychelles, eyes peeled for GTs.

Take a moment to imagine we are walking along a flat. Then, in the distance we see a shark, but something is different about this shark. It seems to be surrounded by … something? It's a dozen sickle tails, wow! Those are all GTs! OK, let's try and keep our cool and get into position, let's try and move closer to the shark. I know it seems crazy but trust me – now, cast the fly in a 30 x 30ft radius within range of the gang of GTs. Nice. Start stripping, strip, strip, strip, faster, strip… they are all coming, strip… *Boom!* Hold on, and turn the drag all the way. How can you not just love that feeling of the fish taking the fly, of its whole head pushing through the water and him looking you straight in the eye, as if to say, this is mine, get your own?! They are the ultimate predator!

Farquhar is special in many ways but just how unique, we were to find out at the beginning of the season in October 2011. With all the pre-season preparation done in less than 48 hours, we set out on the first morning with our clients to see what Farquhar had to offer. We started by heading to our 'go-to' spots. With an early morning high tide we knew that the fishing would be impressive. Trainee guide Rhett and I started off at Depose whilst Keith, a Seychelles veteran, along with fellow guide Warren, set off to Goulette. Having had a great stint on the south-western side of the atoll, smashing some great GTs and bonefish I could not imagine that the fishing could be any better elsewhere on the atoll that morning. Little did I know that my colleagues would come back with a fishing story so crazy that I struggled to believe it.

To cut a long story short, the team that went to Goulette saw explosions of water around the island, particularly in the deeper water on the lagoon side of the island. The guides came to the conclusion that it was GTs hunting either tropical squid or baitfish, both of which we had seen many times before. The clients with Keith made their way to the ocean side of the island while Warren went back to retrieve an additional fly rod from the boat anchored at the back of the lagoon. He stayed with the boat for a bit; trying to work out what exactly was going on.

Goulette is a breeding ground for tens of thousands of Sooty Terns. September to December is the time that the juvenile Sootys learn to fly. There are birds everywhere and it is almost impossible to hear one another above the noise. With all of this chaos going on around him, Warren suddenly saw, out of the corner of his eye, a juvenile Sooty Tern taking off and flying low over the water. Like the great white sharks at False Bay in Cape Town, a GT breached out of the water and swallowed the bird whole. Completely forgetting the fly rod, Warren sprinted

down the beach, so he could share this amazingly ridiculous story with the rest of the crew. In the middle of wrestling with some GTs, the rest of the team weren't able to leave and go and investigate straight away and that night we were all still discussing this phenomenal experience. Mostly the comments were of disbelief, but I can assure you, everyone was thinking what I was thinking – and I was planning to go back there the very next day so we could see for ourselves.

I had very little sleep that night, tossing and turning, thinking about the last time I had guided at Cosmoledo. Then I had witnessed first-hand the moment a GT tried to drown a Booby swimming around on the surface. Could Warren's account of the GT eating a bird be true? I wasn't too sure myself, but I was more than a little interested to find out. That morning, as we readied the boats, you could tell that everyone was still thinking about those GTs. Boats ready, clients aboard, we headed out towards Goulette. I approached the island very stealthy and told my clients that we would fish the ocean side first and then spend the rest of the day focusing on the 'phenomenon'. Once we set foot on the Island, I immediately noticed that the land resembled a war zone: birds with wings missing and quite a large number of injured or dead birds.

We made our way to the southern point of Goulette, where I spotted three monster GTs in the deeper water. I had to shout instructions to my clients over the screaming birds, but they managed to get into position and started casting. The first cast went in and there was no reaction from the

GTs. He loaded the line to cast again and on his forward haul he hooked a bird by accident. The fly and bird landed just a few feet in front of him in the water. That is when we all saw it! Much to our astonishment, a large number of GTs raced over, with one GT crushing the bird in one gigantic gulp! A moment of silence followed as we all just stood there amazed and tried to digest what we had just witnessed. The silence lasted only a few seconds and was followed by some colourful profanity! We went crazy as the fish screamed off, stripping 200 yards of backing in no time. Unfortunately the fish spat out the Sooty and hook after a good fight, but we were definitely not disappointed as we just seen something truly special. Ten minutes later more GTs arrived at the same spot. One cast and we were into another fish, with the fly this time firmly hooked into the strong jaw. On one occasion I saw a GT breach the water to grab the tail of a Sooty. On the third attempt the GT got a good enough hold of the bird and that was it. We continued to smash GTs for the rest of the day, admiring the sheer power and speed of them. When landed, you could run your hand along the stomach and feel how crammed they were full of birds.

The rest of the season was incredible, with good numbers of GTs landed. They continued feeding on the birds all the way through to December and we have seen this happen every season since. But there have also been times when virtually no GTs were found on the flats. On one occasion I ended up chatting to a group of scientists who were geo-mapping. They told us that there was what looked like an oil slick offshore. I set off for closer inspection and there were millions of swimming crabs. We continued smashing the GTs offshore for most of that season. I count myself lucky to have been able to witness these exciting moments.

CHAPTER 21 - HAWAII & PALMYRA ATOLL

MIKE HENNESSEY

Although Hawaii is synonymous with grander blue marlin (over 1,000lb) and now for its Jurassic Park-size bonefish, not many people know about the trevally population. This far-flung series of volcanic islands are the only state of the US away from the American mainland and some believe that Hawaii might be the origin of flyfishing for trevally. There are numerous species of trevally that inhabit these azure waters including GTs, golden trevally, bar jacks, horse eye jacks, bluefin trevally, island jacks and threadfin jacks. In Hawaii, all trevally are called 'Papio' when they are smaller than 10lb, regardless of species. They then graduate to 'Ulua' once they reach respectable size usually then only being GTs or white trevally. Most conventional anglers in Hawaii hike onto high rock structures overlooking incredibly steep drop-offs of over 50 metres deep. Here the waves crash against the cliff faces allowing GTs to roam close to shore. It is an extreme form of fishing and there are casualties every year of anglers blown off the rocks by massive waves or while fighting a big GT.

Mike Hennessey holds a Pacific bruiser

Hawaiian GTs are relatively rare on the flats with sightings on Oahu once a week. Fish from 40lb-80lb can be found marauding the edges of the coral and pancake flats. As the prime target on the Hawaiian flats are the giant bonefish, it can make it hard to justify carrying a GT outfit all the time for that rare occasion the tax collector shows its ugly mug. Although normal procedure if you are wading the flats of Christmas Island or Palmyra Atoll, in Hawaii this just doesn't make logistic sense. Mike Hennessey guides these waters and has taken to casting his bonefish fly at them with some great success and some epic failures. As he is normally fishing heavier than normal bonefish equipment to tackle the monster bonefish, he has found that crab patterns can be very effective.

You would be surprised to know that a 70lb GT will completely forget about herding up a school of mullet on a shelf for a nice crab that's floating with no chance of escape. The trick is to strip strike the second the GT opens its mouth and stick it in the lip. You then have a chance of

the leader holding for an extended period of time. The next issue is the extreme barrier reef that surrounds the flats – then a secondary reef that spills into the ocean. It is a psychological mind game to make the GT think it is pitted against heavier tackle and make it roll over before it realises it could break you off at any moment. Our biggest landed with the small rods is a respectable 40lb GT in water less than 10ft deep which seems impossible. Many times we have seen medium-size GTs actually come on to the flats on their sides, decreasing their depth profile while herding mullet and other baitfish into tidal traps. Eat and run attack patterns like this aren't common but happen about once a week if you know where to look. We have hooked much bigger fish on our bonefish flats but get ruined especially when we are wade-fishing and can't get back to the boat in time before we have to just grab the spool and pop the tippet or risk losing everything.

A more common trevally found on the flats of Hawaii are the stunning golden trevally. These fish are foraging on crabs on the same flats as the bonefish, but also attack bait fish schools on the edges. Golden trevally are in essence a crab-eating GT that grows to 30lb in Hawaii. Where a GT fights with speed and raw strength, a golden trevally will fight dirty and wrap you around coral heads and deep water obstacles once it clears the flat. Tailing golden trevally can be found mixed in tailing with big bonefish on the flats, but are usually found mudding on the edges or back-waking. These bruisers present a fantastic challenge to the flyfisherman incorporating the feeding habits of a permit with the power and aggression of GT. It is important to lead a golden just like a permit, as close as you can without hitting it on the head, which will usually draw a strike the second it hits the water so be ready and tight to strike the moment you land…no slack casting allowed. I call it feathering a cast, which is just letting the line fly through your hand without letting go and lightly breaking your cast near its desired length which will help the roll-over land completely extended and ready to fish with no slack loops…actually this cast should be fished on everything saltwater in my opinion but does take some practice. Golden trevally do have a weak gill membrane so make sure on the release you keep your fingers trapped behind its pectoral fins as an errant finger in the gills could bleed it out.

A CLOSE ENCOUNTER ON PALMYRA ATOLL

Palmyra is not an atoll that many have come across. It is one of the Northern Line Islands (southeast of Kingman Reef and north of Kiribati Line Islands), located nearly due south of the Hawaiian Islands. The nearest major land mass is almost 5,400km to the northeast. The atoll is 12km² with a 14km coastline and has only one anchorage known as West Lagoon. It is owned by the US and was utilised as a forward naval and supply base during the Pacific war where a deep water channel was blown through its coral reef and a landing strip built. After World War

II it was abandoned. Although used as a forward observation site for some of the nuclear testing in the 1950s it remained abandoned until bought by the Nature Conservancy in the 2000. It has since remained in their care as an intact atoll marine eco-system for study. Every so often with special licences fishermen are allowed to help conduct research on the fish populations that inhabit it.

I find it one of the most extraordinary untouched atolls on earth, with many leftover remnants of WWII fortification of the Pacific fleet remaining. Most of these vestiges of Man now look like a tropical apocalypse with nature reclaiming some of the most beautiful flats on earth. We had experienced an eventful morning's fishing tangling with some large bonefish and sampling a little of what this untouched resource had to offer. Suddenly ahead of us there was a GT coming down the flat pushing a three foot wake off its body which could be clearly seen from over 200 metres away. I knew instantly it was a scary GT of record proportions in the middle of hunting mullet, bonefish or anything else that crossed its path. I have seen GTs following blacktip sharks waiting for scraps: this time the blacktips were following the home guard of all GTs.

Sam looked at me with a confused smile and said, 'Holy shit'. I quietly told him to throw his 7# as far as he could behind us and take the 12# I proffered him. We had over 400 yards of backing on a Hatch 11 Plus which I was hoping would be enough to stop this bruiser if we connected. Sam made a perfect 60ft shot out front inside the 30° cone, and popped the fly once … the 'cruising' GT transformed into a 'hell-bent' GT, accelerating so fast the wave off his head actually started to break and make a spray of white water. It was insane and awe inspiring! With its jaws open it

was instantly obvious this fish could have easily swallowed my whole head – and it missed the popper. So much water was forced up and over the GT's head that the popper went with it and so did its eyeballs crossing to look at it go behind him.

Four attacks later both of our legs had turned to jelly and Sam was screaming 'He can't eat it!!' I yelled 'Put your rod underwater and strip the fly into the water!!' Mr GT smashed the popper literally one rod length from the rod tip, exploding water all over us as the hook came tight at the same moment it saw us. Things got extremely violent at this point with line peeling off the reel at an unreal speed –100 yards, 300 yards, 400 yards with full drag and full palm pressure – I remember Sam's feet skidding across the flat as he tried to hold his ground from being pulled off his feet. It was an incredible experience for both of us until the backing sliced on a science buoy in the middle of the lagoon. Sam was pouring sweat and I was pouring out profanity. We still laugh about such an epic memory. Be happy with the eat and be lucky with a catch.

CHAPTER 22 - KANTON ISLAND

LUKE WYSTRA

Kanton, also known as Abariringa Island, derives its name from the New Bedford whaling vessel 'Canton' running aground on its coral reef without the loss of life on March 4th 1854. The British laid claim to Kanton in the 1850s, formally re-asserted by King Edward VIII in 1936, whilst the United States of America made competing claims during the Great Depression era. World War II would see the atoll used as an essential port for naval air transport across the Pacific, holding strategic importance for launching attacks against the Japanese-occupied Gilbert Islands to the west. Kanton's other uses have included US missile tracking station, astronomy, survey and radio communication sites while various scientific studies continue to occur focusing on the endemic terrestrial life, pest eradication and reef health. The previous fishing exploration parties to Kanton Atoll took place in the early to mid-90s by key flyfishing identities such as Jerry Swanson and Randall Kaufman. Kanton Atoll, part of the Phoenix Islands group received World Heritage Status in 2008. Commercial fishing is banned and sport fishing is possible on a case-by-case basis by permit application.

Luke Wystra cradles a long-awaited prize

Kanton lies 2 degrees south of the equator and 171 degrees west, providing for a consistently hot and tropical climate. The lagoon is over 40 square kilometres in area, composed primarily of deeper coral shoals and what would be considered 'small' flats encircling its internal circumference. The exterior of the atoll features a traditional fringing barrier reef that drops quickly to 200 feet in some areas and beyond. This zone features coral bomboras, rocky limestone and the occasional expanse of sand and rock type flats.

Kanton is the northernmost and only inhabited atoll of the eight that comprise the 'Phoenix Islands'. The Gilbert and the Line Islands lie to the west and east respectively. Kanton is not subject to cyclones due to its proximity to the equator, but logistical access points are often hampered by cyclonic activity and turbulent oceanic conditions due to the Convergence zone. Kanton Atoll remains as one of the last havens on earth with no regular and sustainable access, shielded from the modern world. This remoteness, coupled with official World Heritage status, this atoll of Kiribati has one of the healthiest and most virgin eco-systems to still exist on this planet. Conversely, Kanton is at risk of modern man and the industrial world as global climate variables may determine the fate of this ultra-sensitive environment.

Giant trevally patrol here in reckless abandon, devoid of human fear and in staggering numbers. The GT dominates the surf line, lagoon and the only passage of the atoll, located on the western, leeward side. The passage, where current and tidal movement control the lifeblood of the atoll is separated by 'Spam' Island, where only the strongest survive. The passage is Kanton's GT nerve centre.

Turtles, whale sharks, manta rays and dolphins abound in addition to trophy class species such as triggerfish, bonefish, rainbow runner, jobfish, dogtooth tuna, yellowfin tuna, napoleon wrasse and golden and bluefin trevally. Crescent-tails pierce the water's surface at every aspect, colourful parrotfish and black surgeon's mooch along the bountiful flats. Black-tip whalers cruise every inch of Kanton's waters – a true indication that this reef is well and truly in prime health. Napoleon wrasse, another litmus indicator of reef health, exist in what can only be described as plentiful numbers.

Kanton is inhabited by a couple dozen 'caretakers', posted on a rotation basis. The community provides key self-sufficient services such as basic medical and education as well as a police officer, also sharing immigration and biosecurity duties. The community is sustained by religion, the good book maintaining strong bonds and resolve during a relatively uneventful tenure. Access to this jewel of the Pacific is subject to permission and permit only, via the Phoenix Islands Protected Area (PIPA). Current expeditions are supplemented via mother ship vessel that undertake a 680 nautical mile voyage from Western Samoa, the closest serviced port by a substantial factor. On the ground, wading parties are delivered to various parts of the atoll by foot, motorbike, inflatable tender and skiff.

The deserted edges of Kanton Atoll

KANTON BEAST

'Fruits, Fruits, Fruits…?!' Taula's jovial island voice boomed from the galley as I scavenged through my kit at a frantic pace. 'Meat and rice?' he repeated. He would soon realise that I wasn't ignoring him, I was just in a much deeper place focused on the six energetic anglers and a near-overwhelming mental mountain. This journey had grown from a simple idea into a living dream over the last decade. Setting foot on this revered coral atoll has not been without its extraordinary challenges. Rock Expeditions can proudly state that we successfully applied for the first, ratified and granted, catch-and-release sport fishing permit, ever. A government observer also accompanied our expedition to ensure compliance with best practices, at our cost.

The feeling of anticipation for this expedition was like no other. The best part of the last decade was spent working on this project and I was standing at ground zero. Amongst many other trials and tribulations, not only did we make it to Kanton, we were instrumental in overturning a blanket fishing ban. Nothing is ever easy or to be taken for granted in the Pacific. Randall Kaufman bears a certain responsibility for this success; an inspiring article he wrote almost 20 years ago. We were now burning our brand onto the biggest bull on the farm, re-discovering a lost Pacific oasis, Kanton.

Time stood still on the *MV Contraband* as anticipation and anxiousness kept me pacing around the deck in a futile attempt to stay occupied. I re-checked my connections for the umpteenth time. My ears pricked as the sound of the humble little outboard struggled at its limits against eights knots of relentless tidal flow. Our red inflatable appeared from obscurity, passing the final point of the dredged channel and eventually gliding out of the flow into a millpond of a thousand shades of cyan. In my head I recanted stories of my friend Emil of the Gilbert Islands. He would stretch his hands out as far as he could while filling his lungs with air for a little extra reach. 'The GTs there; biggest in the world!' he would exclaim with a gleaming smile.

We were in the process of transporting our anglers to several points along the western aspect of the atoll. I had stayed behind so that the team could get their first cast as the inflatable only carried two people. In a hurry to pack the tender with a proverbial tackle shop of equipment, I had mistakenly made the most cardinal of sins; I forgot the water. Some quick words with the team and we had a plan. Andrew and Bernard would continue exploration, maintaining two-way radio contact, I would pack additional water, food and check in with the topwater guys terrorising giants along the northern foreshore. I knew Andrew was a very experienced angler who had fished Kiritimati countless times, he would be fine to work autonomously. The equatorial sun was red-lining my body temperature, encouraging my penchant thirstiness for Mango Tang.

Finally ready, the tender began the course across the passage, passing behind Spam Island and through the channel. At a tortuous speed, the little tender inched forward. The extra time had allowed me to glance sideways at Spam once more; I then turned to my friend Taula. His expression was priceless, his eyebrows wanting to escape his excited brow with glee. No words were needed and our course changed for a direct route to the leeward side of Spam Island.

Yesterday we had seen two vicious GTs showering petrified sauries and flying fish onto the sand; menacingly forcing the schools hard against the beach. Broad silver bodies and glittering scales hit the broken coral shore. A symphony of splashes and gurgles carried across the water as the vacuous eddies from the broadsiding beasts were refilled; their broaching masses flicking coral onto the beach with clinking crescendo. We were in awe. There are so few places where giant trevally will demonstrate a natural topwater frenzy with complete disregard for the eyes watching.

I jumped off the tender with 12# in hand. A crowbar could not prise this weapon from my tight grip. It was time to put Kanton's GT pedigree to the test for myself. Rounding over the coral escarpment, the full glory of Kanton's passage lay before me. A deep channel some 400 metres wide from the middle island junction. Nutrient-rich electric blue water pushes over countless coral heads, sharply rising to the sandy rubble edge of the island. A gang of charcoal black trevally patrolled effortlessly along the slack edge, pushing in and out of the flow as though it was a regimented routine. A mere twenty foot cast would suffice. Shooting 40 feet and beyond their nose and boisterously back along it. Each fish was 60-100lb and ready to kill, maim or feed. This was no time for buck fever – whatever I would throw was going to get scoffed. This scene would play over and over in my head over the following days.

Taula hooted and hollered with excitement as the GTs showcased their effortless power. A series of figure eights and violent whirlpools scattered across the rushing water; GT are piscatorial depth chargers! 'Blue Valley, Blue Valley!' was Taula's interpretation of what we were calling the GT, having seen very few of them at his native Samoa. Over-fishing, one could only assume.

The fly disappeared into an unnatural mountain of foamy white water, shimmering wide bodies piled on top of each other, their tails slapping the water. The fly was in there somewhere, waiting for its malicious and rapid fate. One more strip and I could keep the game going to even crazier heights… 'Strip!' I yelled.

The Rio line shot forth from the foamy eruption, several broad shoulders and fervent heads in pursuit. The biggest of them all, possibly 100lb (this being a fishing anecdote) claimed what was his, as king, patriarch and keeper of this domain. The fish turned on the Saury imitation in a split second, the hook had found flesh but was not yet set. I fumbled, my sure hands and focus were failing me in the excitement and I struggled to gain traction along the flyline as it disappeared at an unholy rate.

The fish had dispersed and I was left with 40 feet of line caught in the current. The fish had spat out the fly and the 'strip of shame' and subsequent checking of connections followed. I was disheartened but not beaten. Every point on that barren but magnificent island was riddled with GTs that could be sight-casted to at least twice during a tidal window. I could not think of a more depressing place to be born into this world as a baitfish or juvenile Booby bird! Simply stepping foot on Kanton meant that I would never be mentally beaten by a fish in this place. Losing the fish of lifetime on fly; that's just fishing, the sport I love. As a guide, I'm blessed that my chances at a fish of a lifetime are limited only by the skin left on my fingers and a flask of Mango Tang in my pack.

CHAPTER 23 - MOZAMBIQUE

GRAHAM POLLARD

The rolling dunes of Benguerra

The Mozambique coastline stretches 2,500km up the east coast of Africa, bordered by South Africa in the south and Tanzania in the north. The coastline changes dramatically as it journeys northwards and is blessed with a number of beautiful archipelagos and several large rivers – including the mighty Zambezi River – which empty into the Indian Ocean. These islands and rivers make an ideal habitat for fish and anglers to pursue them in.

After almost three decades of war in Mozambique, tourists (and anglers) came flooding back after the peace treaty was signed in the early 90s. Those old enough and lucky enough to have journeyed to Mozambique before the war were responsible for its cult-following which inspired those that hadn't yet had the good fortune of experiencing what it had to offer. The stories of plates piled high with LM (Lourenco Marques) prawns, endless palm-fringed beaches and unexplored fishing grounds had the younger generation yearning for somewhere they hadn't yet seen.

Graham Pollard in his natural environment

The war years meant very little commercial fishing pressure and local subsistence fishing was done with very rudimentary equipment. The visiting anglers, being the least sensible and most eager of the bunch, were the first to venture back in the late 80s even before the war was officially over. The Inhaca and Bazaruto Archipelagos were the first to be visited regularly and a couple of fishing lodges popped up here. One of the species always high on any angler's bucket list is the GT. GTs are abundant up the entire length of the Mozambique coastline and are a trophy fish targeted by conventional and fly anglers alike.

It was at this time that saltwater flyfishing was gaining popularity worldwide and the large numbers of schooling and surface-feeding fish made Mozambique an ideal destination for the first-timer in the salt. During these early days, flyfishing equipment was usually just the heaviest fresh water outfit you owned and although many good fish were caught on 7# outfits with a click and pawl reel, there was a limit to what could be landed.

As saltwater flyfishing gained momentum, fishermen came to see it as a successful way of fishing rather than just some fun to be had when the conditions were right. Specialist saltwater flyfishing equipment was developing and allowed anglers to target larger fish and do so with more success. Once disc drags and 12# outfits became a regular part of the flyfishers' arsenal, a fair bit of success was had blind casting for GTs over the shallow reefs and likely-looking rips with large poppers and big flashy profiles. This is tiring work as long regular casts are required, but the rewards were there to be reaped for those willing to put in the hours.

Even though surface-feeding fish are great sport, there are times of the year when baitfish are few and fish don't feed on the surface as consistently. It was these quiet times where the fish were 'hiding' deeper that led Andrew Parsons and a couple of other guides to develop deep water flyfishing, what is now commonly referred to as dredging. It involves using heavily-weighted clouser minnows and 400-700 grain shooting heads with long running lines to get the fly down to the deep reefs. In calmer weather you have to be careful about hooking the reef in 30 metres of water. Even in windy conditions you can maximise the time your flyline sinks by casting downwind and allowing your fly to sink as the boat drifts over the top.

Dredging is in essence a way of jigging with a flyrod and there are many purists who turn their noses up at it. The truth though is that it is highly effective and a great way to fish when sight fishing isn't possible; either due to bad light, dirty water or uncooperative fish. You also have no idea what fish will jump on your fly as you rip it up from the depths. It just so happens that all of the trevally species, including the GT, are rather prone to this form of flyfishing. The Bazaruto Archipelago in particular is home to large numbers of several hard-fighting trevally species. Pound for pound the bludger trevally and the golden trevally are two of the hardest fighting fish in the sea and we always joke that we're lucky that they don't get any bigger than they do. As dredging takes place over the reef, a hooked GT doesn't have to go too far to cut you off on the reef and without doubt the biggest challenge is stopping the GT before it finds a ledge to cut you off on.

Hook and hold

In the late 80s and early 90s Mozambique was the place many South African flyfisherman went to get their shot of saltwater adrenalin and it played a large part in popularising saltwater flyfishing in Africa. As the political arena changed, the rest of Africa and the world opened up and became more affordable and the move towards flats and visual flyfishing has meant that Mozambique has taken a bit of a back seat.

Having said that, there are many unexplored areas of the Mozambique coastline just waiting to be discovered. There is a strong move towards conservation by both the Government and the fishing lodges up the coast and Mozambique definitely has a bright future from a flyfishing perspective. Mozambique is still the place to go to relax on a beautiful palm-fringed beach, eat a large plate of LM prawns, wet a flyline and with a bit of luck, land that fish of lifetime.

GOLDEN DOUBLE

I had been guiding for a couple of years in the Bazaruto Archipelago and Andrew Parsons returned for a visit. This was a great opportunity for me to catch up with him as well as spend some time with a rod in hand; something as guides we don't get to do as much as we would like. It was midwinter so we had a couple of species in mind. One afternoon found us inside the bay of the Bazaruto Archipelago, slow-drifting in 15 metres of water over a piece of scattered reef that had a habit of holding some good-sized golden trevally.

Bonny (Andrew's girlfriend) had a 10# flyrod rigged with the standard shooting head and 2/0 heavily weighted chartreuse and white clouser. Just as we came onto the reef Bonny had made a short cast and let the fly sink down – I was still letting line out. About three strips into her retrieve Bonny went tight. I could see straight up it wasn't a young fish and I knew that light tackle meant a lot of boat work and chasing, so I started my strip immediately to get my fly out of the water. The fish had other ideas though and one pounced on my fly as soon as I got it moving.

We were now in a bit of a predicament. It appeared that we had two good fish on and both were on pretty light tackle. We did what all fishermen do in such situations and remained overly-optimistic. Things started off pretty well, with both fish headed off in the same direction and neither of them took too much string. It was only about 20 minutes into the fight that my fish seemed to realise he was hooked and made a long run in the opposite direction to Bonny's fish. I wasn't really in the driving seat of this fight and could not put much pressure on the fish. I was rapidly running out of line and desperately praying for my fish to turn. Andrew couldn't do much. If he pushed the boat in the direction of Bonny's fish I was going to get spooled.

Bonny did an excellent job of ramping up the pressure on her fish. The extra pressure paid off and after a half hour fight, Bonny had a lovely golden trevally in the net. With one fish on board we were free to track down my fish with the boat. Golden trevally are an amazingly tough and tenacious member of the trevally family and when targeting them off a boat I have found that, pound for pound, they often pull harder than a GT. I have had many clients attached to good size goldens and even with a 30lb leader they don't seem to want to give an inch. With this in the back of my mind I was wondering how on earth I was going to go about getting this fish to the boat. I was hoping that the fish wasn't too big and that I would start to win a bit of line and get him up in the water column. It wasn't to be. The fish kept taking line and hugging the bottom. I put as much pressure as I dared and didn't seem to be making any inroads.

Andrew kept reassuring me that patience was the key and that we would get this fish if we just kept at it. Of course he was right. Once we got past the hour-and-a-half mark, the fish seemed to finally tire and I managed to lift him off the bottom a couple of times only to have him peel yet more line off and go back to hugging the bottom. Luckily for me, the golden did eventually let up and just short of the two hour mark, the fish broke the surface and Andrew slid the net below him. We slipped the second fish into the opposite fish hatch which Andrew had also filled with water and raced to a tide-exposed sandbank. We did all of this as quickly as we could and then slid the fish back into the water and they swam off as a pair. The two fish weighed in at 19 and 19½ pounds. It was incredible that Bonny's fish had spent the better part of 90 minutes in a water-filled fish hatch and didn't seem any worse off for it.

CHAPTER 24 - OMAN

BRANDON KING

The Sultanate of Oman is situated on the south-eastern side of the Arabian peninsula. It is a country rich in history and from the late 17th century onwards competed with Portugal and Britain for influence in the Persian Gulf and Indian Ocean. At its peak in the 19th century, Oman's influence and control extended across to Iran and Pakistan, and as far south as Zanzibar. In the 20th century the sultanate came under the influence of the United Kingdom. Historically, Muscat (modern day capital of Oman) was the principal trading port of the Persian Gulf region. Oman remains an absolute monarchy and remained relatively hard to access until the 1970s when Sultan Qaboos Bin Said overthrew his father to gain control of Oman. With this power he brought economic reform and modernisation.

Oman's economy is reliant on its oil resources and petroleum products which have been key in the rapid development of the country. Agriculture and fishing remain important sources of income and more recently a fast growing tourism sector has contributed to the economy. Oman has a

largely untouched coastline, rugged unforgiving mountains, beautiful riverbed oasis (or wadis) and vast sand dune-filled deserts. The many towns are steeped in history, with their forts, palaces and walled cities. It is a mystical and special, untouched destination with the most welcoming people you could ever wish to meet.

The 2,092km of coastline is a mixture of long sprawling sandy beaches, covering hundreds of kilometres, secluded rocky bays and sheer jagged cliffs that end dramatically at the ocean. With the Gulf of Oman in the north and the Arabian Sea in the south (a region of the north Indian Ocean) Oman has almost every possible landscape on offer.

Oman has only appeared on the sport fishing map within the last ten years. It has made a name for itself as one of the greatest GT destinations for record-sized fish. These behemoths have so far been targeted by offshore fishermen using heavy spinning gear, poppers and stick baits to entice them, some the size of your forearm. Once hooked up to one of these giants, anglers are often towed around the boat in a brutal tug-of-war, sometimes resulting in the fisherman ending up flat on his back having been broken off or 'reefed'. These fish, usually weighing in around 40-65kg, have been known to reach up to 70kg (150lb). Not an ideal to target on the fly, but that certainly hasn't stopped us trying.

Arabian Fly and Sport fishing was set up to specifically cater to the flyfishing market. Still in its early stages of development, they have explored most of the coastline finding some incredible flyfishing locations; from stalking the miles of beaches in search of Indo-Pacific permit to secluded rocky bays fishing for bluefish, bream, pompano, GTs and a host of other trevally species. Offshore, there is world class bluewater fishing for those wanting to target pelagic species on fly. And who knows what putting a fly in front of many of the bait balls may result in? Milkfish are present in their hundreds, feeding on the surface and they add yet another facet to this versatile region.

THE ONE THAT GOT AWAY

Oman is known for its absolutely massive giant trevally, but these huge beasts have always been targeted from a boat and on conventional popping and spinning gear. Today we were embarking on a new challenge, we wanted to target them from the shore, and, to up the stakes, we were after one of these behemoths on the fly! As they have been known out here to reach up to 70kg, this was going to be no easy feat.

Bluefin trevally against the beach

The beaches of Oman

During my many fishing trips along the coastline over the last five months I had seen some really big GTs race into the shallow waters to smash bait fish when I was walking the shores. Unfortunately, every time I was either without my 12# or I was with clients who were targeting permit with 9# rods. Although it is possible to catch some of the smaller guys on a 9 weight, these had all been 20+kg fish so we wouldn't have had a hope in hell of landing them from the shore.

Arriving at our secluded bay I rigged up my Hardy 12# rod and Abel super 12 reel with a floating line. I had studied these waters, which were usually teeming with bait fish, shad (blue fish), three spot pompano and the occasional permit, during previous visits to this area. I chose a tan EP fibre bait fish pattern as my weapon of choice. Loaded up with extra flies, leader and flyline… just in case…we set off.

Reaching the beach our hearts sank a little as the wind had started to pick up and the waves were now chest high which put paid to any ideas of wading out to the deeper water. We weren't ready to give up though so instead we began to walk the beach, eyes glued just past the breaking waves on the deep dark water. We had some shots at blue fish and three spot pompano to keep us busy, but I always had one eye on the lookout and my 12 weight at the ready. Alas by lunch time we still had not seen a single Geet, so we retired to a 40ft sand dune that gave us a spectacular view of the entire beach and water below.

The wind had picked up even more, whipping the sand around us and into our food…no one likes a gritty chicken salad so we gave up trying to eat lunch and sat staring out to sea. The bait

fish below had become nervous and started to act erratically and looked very uneasy. They had gone from gently gliding along in a tight knit schooling formation, riding the waves as one, to frantic busts of speed shooting off in all directions. Then from nowhere the seas erupted. Two huge dark black shapes had dominated the waters. Like torpedoes they raced in towards shore, creating havoc and scattering bait fish to the left and right, crashing into each other like bullies in a playground, their giant black gaping mouths wide open, inhaling anything in their path.

Leaping up I almost threw myself down the sand dune as I raced towards the water's edge, frantically stripping line as I went. Shouting up to Clare who was now my look-out from above, I started to cast. The waves were big and came crashing around me making it almost impossible to see into the water. All I could do was to release a Hail Mary cast as far past the waves as the wind would allow – and pray. The minute my fly landed just beyond the waves, I started to strip. It was all quite surreal for me as there had been an instant role reversal. Going from guiding other people to now being guided was a new challenge for me. Above me on the sand dune, Clare was shouting orders to cast, cast, strip, strip, go left, no, right…move it! I could see the two fish now, like dark sinister figures surfing in towards the shore on the back waves and smashing bait fish, but they were just out of reach... God this was frustrating! Then for a split second the wind seemed to die down slightly and the two Geets came crashing hungrily towards the shore.

'Cast, Cast, one o'clock… now!' came my instruction from above. Punching the line through the wind I watched the fly land just three feet from the lead fish. Black as night, it angrily accelerated towards my fly with the second fish hot on his tail, giant mouth wide open as it chased after my fly. My heart was in my mouth as I frantically stripped the line in. The end of my flyline was now in sight, with just a few feet before it reached my rod tip and the fish was bearing down fast. His nose was now almost on my fly, and then…nothing. In the blink of an eye he screeched on the brakes, turned away and slunk off into the deep blue with his mate hot on his tail. What the…? I stood staring in disbelief at they disappeared into the ocean, flyline at my feet and my fly now dangling like an old sock in the white water around me.

All I could hear from above were howls of laughter and a little voice shouting… 'Now you know how your clients feel when they don't connect!' Grrrrrr… this had turned from a challenge into a personal vendetta, I was going to get one of these big bad boys…just maybe not today!

CHAPTER 25 - PROVIDENCE ATOLL, SEYCHELLES

GERHARD LAUBSCHER

Of all the atolls in the Seychelles, Providence is the most unique. The topographical structure of the atoll is different from all the others in the Seychelles and creates a unique and often misunderstood habitat for a plethora of fish species.

Whilst all the atolls in the Seychelles, and for that matter the Indian Ocean, are essentially home to the same species of fish, different atolls suit different species better. If you look at the topography of the different atolls on Google Earth, Providence Atoll immediately stands out. Unlike all of the other atolls in the Seychelles, Providence does not have a major channel draining the lagoon. St Josephs, St Francois, Alphonse, Farquhar, Cosmoledo, Astove and Aldabra all have at least one dominant channel draining the lagoon on the inside of the atoll. This channel helps to push cold water into the lagoon and onto the flats of the atoll. Providence doesn't have a channel like this, thereby creating a unique and different eco-system.

The edge of North Island, Providence Atoll

The lack of a main drainage channel means that there can, from time to time, be more stagnant water on the atoll. This stagnant water often heats up creating the perfect environment for turtle grass to grow in. For the fly angler this has two major implications, one big disadvantage and one big advantage. The disadvantage is the turtle grass makes it very difficult to see fish, the dark bottom hides fish easily. Unlike on a powder-white sand bottom, the fish doesn't stand out. The advantage is that the turtle grass creates a habitat which holds a large number of prey items predatory fish like to feed on. The turtle grass flats are rich in life and can draw huge numbers of predatory fish.

However, it gets more confusing…the most important factor fly anglers fishing Providence have to keep in mind is that we are always looking for cold water in our quest to find fish on the flats. When the water on the flats gets stagnant it can become very hot and species like GTs tend to avoid this warm water like the plague. It is for this reason that we focus our efforts on Providence

Atoll over the fringe season when the weather is more unstable. During the unstable weather, the wind and periodic rains helps to keep the water on the flats cold and there is a major increase in the number of game fish we find on the flats. This makes for more challenging fishing conditions but, just like at so many other fishing destinations, the fishing is much better!

THE RETURN TO PROVIDENCE

It was one of those mornings that felt the way you imagine it would when you look at a picture. By the time we moored the tender boat on the southern tip of Cerf Island I had beads of sweat streaming down my face. The air was still relatively cool but the morning sun was already beating down on us and the lack of wind made it even worse.

I looked down towards the southern tip of the atoll. The surface was like the proverbial mirror and the only distinction between the horizon and the ocean was the faint white line of breaking waves crashing into the edge of the atoll. If it weren't for the surf break it would have been a continuous mirage, impossible to define where the sky begins and the water ends.

This section of the atoll can best be described as a drowned desert, it's a two mile section of underwater sand dunes. Sandy channels and knolls stretch down as far as the eye can see creating a myriad of different currents, ridges and channels. The overcast weather from the previous couple of days combined with the favourable winds played in our favour. The water was cool and a clear blue colour; we couldn't ask for more ideal conditions on one of the most unforgiving atolls in the Indian Ocean. We were on a falling tide and the plan was to wade down towards the surf zone along with the receding tide in the hope of finding some GTs falling off the flats along with the tide. But we never made it to the surf zone, we didn't even come close.

When the tide was low enough for us to wade we started heading towards the south, sticking to the apices of the underwater sand dunes. I spotted the first fish seconds after entering the water, it was a solitary fish of about 15lb holding stationary in the current. The fish was 30 yards away from us, sitting in a current break created by the sand dunes and holding a stationary lie similar to where you would expect to see a salmonid holding in a big river. We position ourselves upstream and slightly across from the fish and James made the cast. The fly landed and swung in towards the fish, a textbook presentation. As the fly came into its field of vision it simply lifted from the bottom and accelerated towards the fly, smashing it in one smooth movement and James set the hook. A short while later we landed and released the silver torpedo. As he swam off I looked up and I could not believe what I saw. As far as I could see behind every current break there was a stationary GT holding.

We walked from fish to fish and caught just about every single one, starting with the 'upstream' fish and working our way down, trying to make sure that the hooked fish would not spook any of the other fish around it. It was like fishing a spring creek using a 12# rod and 6/0 flashy profiles. None of the fish were monsters, the biggest being maybe 25lb, but it was one of the most perfect GT sessions I have ever fished. The sessions continued for as long as the tide was falling. As we approached lunchtime we had caught just about every fish we could see and the tide was now too low. The session was over and we made our way back to the mother ship for a well-deserved lunch.

The air-conditioned environment of the mother ship, lunch and some cold drinks over the stagnant low-tide was the perfect platform on which to 'recharge' our batteries for the afternoon session. We were moored on the western side of the atoll and the plan was to fish the pushing tide in from the cuts in the reef about a third of the way up the atoll.

No horizon day

We could not have timed it more perfectly. When the tender boat dropped us in the shallow surf zone we were immediately surrounded by sharks. Their movements were erratic in the cold water, pushing in on the rising tide and I called my anglers to stay close to me. The sharks were clearly in feeding mode which was a good sign for us but none-the-less meant we should be careful. We started wading towards shallow water. The difference between the knee depth water we were heading towards and the thigh depth water we now found ourselves in were crucial. The sharks would seldom venture into the knee-depth water yet it was the ideal depth from which to spot GTs and the anglers could still move relatively quickly to intercept spotted fish.

We hadn't reached the knee-depth water when Rob spotted the first fish and pursued it. GTs suddenly appeared from all directions, we were surrounded by them and within seconds all the anglers were hooked up. The tide kept pushing us up the flat as the guests caught and landed one GT after the next. They were bigger than the fish of the morning session, typical Providence fish with big girths, mostly in the 30lb range. The session was shorter than the morning sessions but more intense. I spent all my time on shark patrol as I walked between the anglers landing and unhooking one GT after the next. We photographed one or two fish but the action was just too hot to spend time on photographing fish, plus with all the sharks around I wasn't too keen to be holding onto fish for extended periods of time.

There are small drainage channels that cross the flats linking the complex lagoon system in the middle of the atoll to the surf zone on the eastern edge. The majority of GTs had passed us, crossing into the lagoon system where they would probably spend the majority of the tide hunting. As we headed up one of these channels I spotted a commotion on a section of turtle grass flat. We walked closer and as if the day hadn't been good enough, Providence showed us one of her true treasures, tailing GTs!

The pack of about eight fish were working an area roughly the size of a small bedroom, tailing hard on the turtle grass, foraging for whatever crustaceans and baitfish were seeking cover in the turtle grass bank. The fish were so occupied in finding their prey that we walked to within 40 feet of them before starting the casts and simultaneously dropping two flies into the pack of feeding fish. The anglers let the flies sink for a couple of seconds to get them to the eye level of the fish before starting the retrieve. Within seconds we had a double hook-up. In typical fashion the fish peeled off but the pre-set drags on the 12# reels stopped them before they got too far and we soon landed two 30lb fish.

The session ended as abruptly as it began. Soon the water was too deep and I radioed for the tender boat to come and collect us. In total we landed 33 GTs that day. No real monsters, but it was a perfect session. We caught fish holding stationary lies, off the back of sharks, cruising in the surf zone, tailing on turtle grass flats and hunting in small packs. We saw just about everything any GT angler could ask for.

CHAPTER 26 - ST BRANDON'S, MAURITIUS

TIM BABICH

St Brandon's (Cargados Carajos Shoals) is a small piece of paradise situated 268 nautical miles north-east of Mauritius in the Indian Ocean and to date is only accessible by ship. The atoll itself consists of over 50 small islands, coral ridges and vast sand flats which extend 50km from north to south taking up an area of no less than 190km². The discovery of the atoll is unclear, but may have been visited as early as 600AD by Arabian sailors. Portuguese sailors however named it in 1506 when they came across it on their way to India, after which the Dutch occupied the atoll in 1598. The islands became a French protectorate in 1722 and then passed over to the British in 1810. Like so many other islands of the Indian ocean, St Brandon's was mined for its guano, which stopped in the mid-twentieth century. To this day the island is classified as a dependent of Mauritius and for many years non-Mauritians were banned from visiting her shores. Thankfully the red tape has been cleared and with the right paperwork and permits foreigners can now legally visit this relatively untouched atoll. This is the main contributing factor to its late introduction to the flyfishing world, only becoming a viable option five years ago.

Tim Babich with a specimen St Brandons GT

Though it has had only a short time in the limelight, St Brandon's has become famous for its abundance of large bonefish, Indo-Pacific permit and now is regarded as a world class fishery. St Brandon's is one large atoll with the bulk of fishing taking place in the northern part of the atoll, with the two mentioned species being the main target. In our early days out on the atoll very little time, if any, was spent pursuing the legendary GT. Brief encounters with GTs would occur while anglers went about wading the shallow water looking for bones and permit. In reality this hindered the full exploration of this massive atoll as a large proportion of the time was spent in an area more conducive to classic bone fishing. There are still parts of the atoll that remain unexplored which in today's world is rare and almost unheard of. For those that guide there, it opens up new horizons as with every season a little bit more of what this atoll has to offer is sampled.

Each season that has passed, the guides have slowly started to get their heads around the movements and habits of these 'Gangsters of the Flat' in relation to tides and weather and in doing so have discovered a hidden resource of GTs. In short they have discovered a GT fishery unlike any other encountered before, not in way of numbers of fish like the waters of the Seychelles, but in the size of the GTs that frequent these flats. As an indication, most fish that measure over the magical one metre mark are considered a trophy in the world of flyfishing. With most destinations these larger fish will spend the bulk of their time in deeper off-shore reefs, only venturing onto the flat on certain tides and conditions. At St Brandon's these big ocean-going fish frequent the flats on a daily basis. This frequent behaviour is based around an abundant and forever-present food source – bonefish. This food source is also one of the main contributing factors to the bigger average size of the GTs encountered. One can just imagine the weight gained from eating 6-8lb bonefish which are picked off as and when the GTs please.

Searching...

RAGING TORRENT

I have lost count of the GTs I have had the pleasure of coming face to face with on St Brandon's and there are many stories of battles lost and won. But in saying that there is one fish that comes to mind that I caught a couple years back off the eastern edge of the atoll. The guides refer to this as the wild side of the atoll, reason being the prevailing wind which relentlessly pounds this side of the coast, causing a mess of large waves and strong currents. The conditions faced when fishing this area are tough, to say the least – but as most will know when it comes to GTs, this is often water they seek.

The area I found myself in this particular day had probably never seen a human before, let alone one carrying a flyrod. This is generally the type of scenario I like to find myself in. While slowly moving along the surf line with the tender I could see in the distance a cluster of exposed coral heads half in and half out the water; it was the only form of structure around for miles. At this stage the tide was heaving in from the ocean side and the current was ripping past these newly-discovered coral heads. At a closer inspection I noticed big black shapes in front and behind the coral heads and I quickly realised that they were GTs. With what felt like one flowing movement I shut down the outboard and dropped the anchor.

Running the surf

I jumped up onto the hatch to get a better view and at a first glance I counted about forty fish. They were just holding in the slack water provided by the structure, in the same way a trout would hold in a river. The only difference is that these trout were 100lb plus and had seriously bad attitudes! It was at this stage I saw some movement up-current of the GTs. It was a school of baitfish battling to swim in the current and they had got to the stage where they were dropping back towards the coral heads in order to find shelter and get out of the raging torrent. Little did they know what was waiting for them and as they fell unsuspecting into this trap, all hell broke loose. There were a mass of bait fish bodies flying in every which direction. To be honest I don't think any of them made it out alive and once the slaughter was over, the GTs all moved back into position as if nothing had happened. It became very clear that the GTs weren't there because they wanted to get out of the current, they were there because everything else wanted to get out of the flowing inferno. (Out of the frying pan, into the fire!!) All they had to do is wait and the food would come to them; the prime lie, so to speak! Well with this new-gained knowledge I decided the next unsuspecting bait fish to venture into this death trap would be my fly. Armed with my 12 wt Loomis loaded up with James Christmas NYAP (Not Your Average Popper) I jumped off the boat to make my way out towards the GTs. It quickly became apparent the full extent of the current and I was pretty tired once I had reached my position within casting range up-stream of the mass of GTs.

I readied myself and made the cast at a 45 degree angle and allowed the current to swing the fly into the fish, almost like you would do with a salmon. Once the fly was in range of the school I gave it one single pop. The entire gang of GTs made their way out to investigate this potential food source and all it took was one more pop to trigger the onslaught of open gaping mouths.

One of the bigger fish managed to shoulder its way in first and I saw the trademark black eye balls as the fish raised its head out of the water to engulf the fly. I quickly stepped back at the same time setting the hook, which in turn upset the fish and he made off at a rate of knots. Within seconds I was deep down into my backing as it used the strong current to his advantage. The rest of the school was dazed and confused and were at this stage just swimming around me.

One of the fish had the cheek to give me a nip on my leg just to see if I was edible. Luckily for me they decided against it and left me alone. The same however was not the case for the GT on my line. Once I had managed to gain some line and the fish was now in sight, the rest of his kin rushed him and began attacking this now distressed fish. I managed to wrestle the 115cm beast away from her so-called friends. Once in hand, the other fish just made their way back to the coral heads to take up their positions again, I quickly got some photos taken and gave the fish a chance to recover and let her on her way to fight another day. In reality I could have caught a bunch of them that day but I was satisfied with this beautiful fish. We went our separate ways and I left them, content in the knowledge I would see them there again!

CHAPTER 27 - NUBIAN FLATS, SUDAN

ROB SCOTT

The distinctive Nubian Flats

The Nubian flats are one of the newest flats destinations to burst onto the scene. Although primarily a trigger fishery, it has proved over its first two seasons to have a substantial number of trevally living along its 300 mile virgin coastline. Although perhaps not a country one would associate with saltwater flyfishing, this massive country has a substantial border with the Red Sea. When the current operation was running their exploratory trips, they knew that there would definitely be GTs in those waters, but they had no concept if they would ever become a viable species to target. Sudan is one of the largest countries in Africa and spans some 1,400km across. Not to be confused with South Sudan, which is a separate and troubled country, Sudan itself has been a tourist destination for over a decade. Directly opposite Saudi Arabia, the coastline spans from Egypt all the way south to Eritrea and contains innumerable islands, flats and pinnacles surrounded by some of the clearest oceans and the best diving in the world. This coastline is, for the most part, deserted, as it is the Nubian Desert inhabited by nomadic populations of camel and goat herders with no fishing communities. This is key, as there is no commercial subsistence

Rob Scott after a hard-won battle

fishing apart from a handful of small open boats using hand lines. The fishing pressure is effectively nil.

Fishing for GTs in Sudan is categorised into two different scenarios: flats and drop-offs. Both are different to other fisheries, as the Red Sea has almost no tidal flow. The tidal coefficient is extremely low with the tidal difference often only 10-20 centimetres. On initial exploratories it made it extremely hard to know where and when the GTs would appear. Initially the shots were very rushed and the resulting conversion rate was very low. But with more time and more experience, the ability to know which areas we might find GTs grew. The number of fish landed increased dramatically. The wind is really the only factor to consider, which creates surf. If there is no wind, there is no surf line which takes a little getting used to. From a fishing perspective this unique phenomenon changes the dynamic on the flats, allowing full sessions on the flats without being chased off by rising water. It also allows anglers to walk across the flats and fish right off the coral edged drop-offs which is rare.

On these flats in Sudan, fishing is as pure as any GT fishing across the world. GTs are spotted cruising across coral edge flats or the huge white sand flats that Sudan is renowned for. These fish are either big singles or small groups, on rays, sharks, or turtles. The Nubian flats are also littered with small islands, some with undercut cliffs like those in the Indian Ocean. A walk along these iconic red cliffs provides the perfect vantage point from which to spy GTs going about their daily macabre business. Fighting GTs from these high vantage points is incredibly visual as anglers battle to keep them on the flats before they can either make their way down to the fish or the GT finds the edge or a coral bommie and cuts the line, ending the battle. The bigger the GT, the wiser they seem and the big fish almost always head straight for bommies.

The second way that these iconic fish are targeted in Sudan is a little different to the flats fishing. Although not a favourite amongst some anglers it is extremely productive and that is to tease fish in the bluewater. In some areas in Sudan, the GTs hold on massive drop-offs, where the flat gives way to blue ocean, often in a spectacular sheer drop of a couple hundred metres. With the lack of surf, this allows the unique opportunity to actually fish bluewater while standing on the flats. In point of fact this season a dogtoothed tuna was actually landed on fly from shore. The hookless plug, or tease, is cast far out and retrieved at high speed, often while GTs and other predatory fish turn the ocean white around the teaser as they attempt to destroy the offering.

Once the GTs are within casting distance, the anglers have to make a pin-point accurate cast, so that the GT diverts its attention from the tease to the fly. All of this is extremely visual and happens at lightning speed. For anyone who considers it unfair, it takes a huge amount of skill from the guide and guest team. Everything has to happen perfectly and it takes nerves of steel from the angler to make sure that his skills are up to the test. The GTs of the Nubian Flats will find any crack in your armour. These coral edges can be treacherous wading and some crumble under-foot. As there is no constant push of water over the coral it also has a build-up of algae that is very slippery and why the guides here wear felt-soled boots instead of traditional flats boots. Hooking one of these Sudanese beasts requires a frantic scramble to the edge with your guide to prevent being cut off immediately before engaging in the fight of your life, quite literally on the edge.

THE EDGE

Finding and figuring out the GTs of the Red Sea and the Nubian Flats has been an incredible journey. There have been so many great fish caught that it becomes harder and harder to remember each and every one. Ironically, the two that stick out the most when I look back over the exploratory process are two fish that left us battled and bruised.

The first incident was on our very first trip to explore the coast of Sudan. We hadn't even dubbed the name Nubian Flats. That particular morning had us jumping out on a new island with absolutely zero idea of what we might find. Keith Clover had leapt off the tender boat and while others organised their gear, he walked over a short incline to survey the surrounding coral bommie field. As he ascended the slight incline he shouted 'GTs!' He madly stripped off line from his 12#, made a quick cast and a small GT exploded onto his fly as it hit the water. The other three GTs that were cruising with this fish were all trying to 'steal' the fly out of the hooked GT's mouth. Unfortunately the hook pulled and all four headed off amongst the coral bommies.

By this time a couple of us had joined Keith at the top of the sand dune. Keith wasn't that happy the fish had popped off, but we were all excited about the prospect of the day ahead. As we casually chatted, another of the party began windmilling his arms and yelled 'GT!' From our vantage point we could clearly see a GT between 110 to 120cm cruising over the bommies, obviously attracted by the fuss the smaller fish had made. The behemoth was less then 15 metres

from us, so Keith made a cast, leading the fish by a good 10 metres to ensure it didn't spook. By its body language it was obvious that he saw the fly, although uncharacteristically he didn't explode onto the fly, but meandered in that direction. Keith gave one long steady strip, and the GT slowly swam up to the fly and engulfed it, much like a large mouth bass. Then all hell broke loose and what ensued was a tug-of-war like no other. Keith realised he only had metres to play with and against all odds managed to keep the line clear of all the razor-sharp coral.

After five minutes he had managed to thread the fish past all the bommies and another five metres would have it safely in the clear. I exclaimed that he had it, the fish was in the clear! As the words left my mouth I had cursed the situation and the leader found the last little piece of jagged sharp coral and the fish was gone. That's the thing with GTs, you never know how it is going to turn out!

The second incident occurred early in the first exploratory season. Mark Murray, our head guide for our Tanzanian Tiger and Gabon operations, had joined us for his first taste of flats fishing. Mark has since had three years of guiding on the Nubian Flats under his belt, but at this point he had yet to lay his eyes on a single GT. It was the first day after he had arrived early in the first session. Mark and I were walking a flat edge and were hoping to fish for bohar, bluefin, barracuda; and of course GTs. The modus operandi for the session was to pull these predatory fish out of the deep water to within casting distance on the tease. The particular flat edge gave away to a very foul rocky drop-off, so to ensure that our flylines lasted longer than two minutes we were walking past this section to an area that gave us a better chance of landing a big fish.

As we were walking I scanned the blue and laid my eyes on an absolute monster of a GT, well over a metre. The fish was cruising on the surface of the blue water approximately 150 metres

Battle on the Edge

from the edge of the flat. As with any GT fishing, things have to happen quickly to make sure you capitalize on the chance. Simultaneously I screamed at Mark to get ready with his 12# while I ran to the edge preparing the teasing stick. Mark needed no encouragement, but he was looking in the wrong place. As he came to my side I asked him if he was ready. He said 'My drag is locked and loaded, I am ready to go but I can't see the fish.'

I replied 'Don't worry, it will come behind the tease. Take a couple of deep breaths because this is one giant of a GT.'

With that I cast the teaser out over the blue and started skittering the hookless surface plug back towards us across the surface. Normally GTs explode on the teaser instantly, but on this occasion there was nothing. Just a hookless teaser skimming across the ocean surface. All the time I was screaming, 'Get ready! Get ready!' and Mark was shouting back at me, 'There is no fish, there is no fish!' As the teaser came within range, I yelled at Mark to cast. He made a short cast and as the black semper hit the water, he started to strip. By this stage the teaser was literally 3 metres from us, and as I pulled the teaser out the water, with still no sign of him, my heart sank in the sudden realisation he wasn't coming in.

Mark made the last strip on his flyline, and he started to pull the line back for another cast. As the fly accelerated, a huge black shadow came into view. The 100lb plus GT slammed his fly and simultaneously launched its entire body into the air, not even a metre in front of Mark. It was so close that the splash from the fish left Mark drenched. The fish was deep into the backing within seconds, with Mark applying *maximum* pressure. A couple more split seconds and he found the reef, obliterating the 12# flyline. Mark was clearly more than shaken as he reeled in what was left of his shredded flyline. If ever there was a proper introduction to GT fishing, that was it. These fish can put you in your place very quickly, no matter how prepared or skilled you are.

CHAPTER 28 - CHRISTMAS ISLAND (KIRITIMATI), KIRIBATI

TIM PASK

Considered the largest atoll in the world, Christmas Island is about as far away from civilisation as you can hope for. What many don't realise is that this tiny pin-prick of land in the central Pacific has a long and distinguished history. Discovered by Captain Cook in 1777 it was then utilised by the British to test atomic weapons in the 1950s, closely followed by the Americans in the 1960s. As the local population was evacuated at the time, the island bears remarkably few side-effects, albeit the footprint of the British Army's engineers is still in evidence through buildings and the primitive road structure on the island. The island was also one of the first 'international' saltwater flyfishing destinations and today, over 30 years later, still draws anglers from around the world. The island is serviced by weekly flight on Fiji Airways from Fiji and Honolulu to Cassidy International Airport and the islanders are supported by a monthly cargo ship bringing in much-needed food and supplies.

The island is part of the Line Islands and located 2,150km and 3½ hours flying time south-

Tim Pask with a Silver stunner

west of Honolulu and 230km north of the equator. It is where many of our modern saltwater fishing methods were conceived. At 390 square kilometres, most of the Seychelles atolls would fit comfortably inside the lagoon three times over. At over 20km across, the entire lagoon is a veritable spider's web of flats, channels and islands offering anglers huge opportunity at many species. The current population at last census was just over 5,000 people, centred around three main settlements: London, Tabwakea and Banana. The original settlement of Paris on the other side of the lagoon has since been abandoned. The local population encapsulates everything best about island life: extremely friendly and delighted to share their world with you. On an island where just surviving, finding potable water and the nearest source of modern equipment is 2,900km away, life can be a challenge – which they take in their stride. Despite this, four fishing operations run relatively efficiently with guides and boats to take fishermen onto the flats. Gilbertese is the principal language spoken on the island and the name Kiritimati is pronounced kiri-si-mass as a Gilbertese respelling of the word Christmas.

From the mouth of the Burgle channel next to Cook Island right to the shelves and drop-offs at the back of the lagoon, GTs can be hunted as they patrol their routes looking for food. On the south-east coast a beach line of 80km stretches all the way to the iconic 'Korean Wreck' offering one of the most perfect environments to hunt GTs. The high beach line drops down to a coral edge of some 300 metres that then drops off into the dark abyss. Large ocean bonefish, football-sized triggers and milkfish are prevalent in this area, and so are their pursuers. A long ride down from the inhabited areas, the 'wreck' as it is now known can only be fished effectively on certain tides, but is well worth the trip.

As some who have ventured to her shores have said, it was the numbers and size of bonefish that attracted them, but it is the trevally that make them return. It was here on this far-flung Pacific paradise that modern GT flyfishing was first recorded, and the fraternity of Christmas Island guides focused their attention on them as a fly species. These guides studied their behaviour and had great success with their clients on what we would now consider primitive tackle. If you are looking for somewhere with WiFi and rental cars, this is not it. If however you are looking to fish an extraordinary destination where the pace of life is relaxed and has changed little in the last 40 years, then Christmas Island should be on every flats angler's hit list.

THE LAND OF GIANTS

Everything had unfolded rather quickly, with me standing on the edge of the drop-off looking for cruising bonefish when I caught sight of movement off my right shoulder. I glanced up to see a sea monster coming right at me. I did what came naturally: screamed like a schoolgirl and tried to run. Obviously I was in a couple of feet of water, so I wasn't really running, more like flailing. When I turned back towards the edge I found myself face to face with a great beast that had followed me onto the flats. Another blood-curdling scream was followed by the now infamous double-handed swing of the flyrod towards the beast.

I didn't tell any of my fishing partners about that encounter as I could not begin to imagine the amount of rip-take I would be given. I did however make up some hellish lie about how I had broken my rod and then spent most of the time in the middle of the bonefish flat, where the fishing was not as good, but it was much safer. That was February 1995 and I was a long way from the trout streams of Montana… and these were definitely not trout.

Once I decided I was committed to catching GTs, my days became easier: well, at least they had focus. I tracked down any guide who would talk to me about GTs and finally found Tebaki, who at that time was the head guide at the Captain Cook Hotel. I pleaded my case and he was all over it. His eyes matched mine in intensity and I knew I was headed in the right direction. He was full of ideas and soon my education began. He explained to me that the giants hunted the rising tides and would follow them all the way to the back of the lagoon on the largest tides. They often travelled in groups and it was not uncommon to see as many as eight huge fish together. When they were focussed on hunting they were virtually fearless and would actually fight for a well-placed fly.

So with 10 weight in hand, off we went. I had gathered from most people that poppers were the best flies to use and had bought a variety of epoxy-style flies in a variety of colours. We hired a boat for the two of us and headed towards the back of the lagoon, trying to catch the rising tide in the morning. I soon found myself stationed on a point where Tebaki had told me GTs often hunted. I was amazed that once I started looking around I could actually see the tide transitioning this area and it was coming alive. Huge bonefish came flying out of the drop-offs and quickly darted back to the safety of the deeper water. Baitfish were quickly schooling up and being pushed towards the tiny point and they leapt in all directions as barracuda, queenfish and who knows what else patrolled the area.

Simon Corrie punches a line into the surf

Tebaki was a great teacher in those early days and he kept me entertained with small talk about the island, its people, his family and pretty much anything he figured would keep me distracted and not moving around. I remember being so entranced by the conversation that I nearly wet myself when he calmly said, 'Tim, there is a giant trevally coming. It is 35 yards at two o'clock, can you see him?' I can honestly tell you that his calmness is what probably saved me from having a stroke. Once again here I was, face to monster face with my prey, only I wasn't sure which one of us was the real prey. I managed to get the fly moving, but had no real chance of getting it in front of me, let alone towards the fish. In my excitement I must have begun moving my feet (you know, the coveted body-lunging style of casting) and this time, instead of charging me, he quickly changed directions and was… gone?

I folded like a cheap lawn chair. I was horribly embarrassed and could hardly talk. I didn't know what to do and was sure I had missed my one opportunity. To my surprise Tebaki just picked up our conversation where it left off, with the exception of some much-needed coaching. 'Tim, please peel off at least 20 yards of line and make some large coils you can hold in your left hand. Then shake some more line out of your rod tip and hold the fly in your right hand.' Then he drifted into some small talk followed by more instructions. This time I kept my eyes focused on the task in hand, but continued to listen as well. 'When the GT comes I want you to cast the fly off at an angle in the direction you see him swimming and then wait. I'll tell you when to strip'.

This time I saw them first (no idea how!) and there were several. I just began casting as soon as I saw them and Tebaki resumed his calming coaching approach. This time the fly landed to the right side of the giants and I could hardly stop immediately stripping. We stood there for what seemed like hours as they approached and it wasn't until they were a short distance from the fly that he told me strip.

No sooner had the fly began to move then every fish tracked the movement and rushed the fly. I was stripping with all the speed I could muster and it wasn't even a close race. They were crashing all over it and water was flying in all directions. I could not even see the fly at this point and they all seemed to be missing it, but then it tightened up. Tebaki actually showed some emotion and yelled, 'Set the hook, set the hook!' With my left arm hand I strip set while my right arm swung low and to the right. The hook held fast and then it happened. The fish disappeared with all my flyline and then hundreds of yards of backing melted away. My newly acquired Billy Pate Tarpon reel was screaming for relief. None came!

Bucket mouth

CHAPTER 29 - SOUTH AFRICA

BEN PRETORIUS & ANDY COETZEE

Kosi Bay

South Africa has a rugged and hostile 3,100km coastline and is bathed by two different oceans and currents on our east and west coast. At the tip of South Africa's Cape Peninsula, the cold Benguela current of the west coast meets the warm and powerful Agulhas current of the east coast. It is a unique phenomenon where such a narrow strip of land separates oceans that are so different in temperature and the life they support.

From a GT flyfishing perspective, it is the warm sub-tropical waters of Indian Ocean on the north-east Maputaland coastline where these fish are most likely to be encountered on fly at venues such as The Mouth at Kosi Bay, Bhanga Nek, Rocktail Bay, Lala Nek, Cape Vidal and Mission Rocks.

Due to the close proximity of the high speed Agulhas current to this rugged coastline, combined with the strong seasonal prevailing winds, the surf and weather conditions are at times some of the

Andy Coetzee with a black surf fish

most testing in the world. Powerful wave action, strong winds and currents, will at times defy the skills of any competent fly angler. It is however the immense satisfaction of landing one of these fabled gamefish on fly from the rock and surf zone that keeps fly anglers going back for more.

To put this into perspective, to the best of my knowledge, to date only twelve fish measuring over 1m fork length (a fish of approximately 20kg plus) have ever been landed from the South African rock and surf zone on fly.

Most of the bays along our Maputaland coast are shielded by rock promontories that lie on a north/east axis relative to the coast. Ideal fishing conditions prevail when strong winds blow from the south-west. Big waves are formed and coupled with the wind create very fast moving and turbulent water at these points/promontories, whilst leaving the water in the lee of the point relatively calm and protected. During the rise and fall of a spring tide you are most likely to

encounter GTs in these fast-flowing and turbulent rip currents. To add spice to this already daunting task, your chances of success are further enhanced whilst fishing in the dark or in very low light conditions and safety devices such as personal floatation devices are the order of the day. All this, while you are casting 6/0-8/0 flies on 12# rods for extended periods. Fun? No, this is really hard work, but it is always undertaken with the possibility of that Holy Grail!

MONSTER GT AND KIDS – ANDY COETZEE

My most memorable encounter with the surf zone bullies was at Rocktail Bay Lodge in December 1998, whilst my young children, Grace (10) and Tom (8) were snorkelling with me. We had launched the fishing ski and ventured to Rocktail Point about 200m offshore. Whilst snorkelling and diving using only masks and fins we were suddenly surrounded by a huge shoal of the giant trevally, all in the 30-40kg class; real bruisers and scared of nothing. Tom was very anxious and clung apprehensively to my shoulders whilst Grace hung onto my back as we slowly circled the shoal, watching them as they peered at us with saucer size eyes and those long flared pectoral fins. What a sight! Tom asked if they were dangerous and my reply said it all: 'Sure Tom, but not to us, only to every other smaller fish in the ocean!'

They are the *real* apex predators of the surf zone, hunting and marauding in the surf, decimating shoals of mullet, shad, bonefish, moonies, and anything that looks like food. I was wildly excited as the promise of a spectacular afternoon's fishing for these brutes was a possibility. After an exhilarating 20 minutes swimming and diving with the bullies, they moved off northwards, probably terrorising every baitfish along the coast. The following morning, with clear images of those GTs seared into my memory, I was up early and woke both the kids to join me at the bay on the high tide at 3.30am. Now that is early for kids, so Tom opted to stay in bed. Grace stumbled down the beach with me as I urged her to speed up, knowing that the fire was burning in my belly to throw a fly or popper at some kingfish. I rigged the flyrod as I walked, stripping basket banging annoyingly against my thigh and dragging poor Grace with me as fast as possible for a 10-year-old to jog; I just knew that the GTs were there. Mullet were flapping on the sand, desperately trying to escape as the GTs were charging up the sand bar on their sides clubbing mullet and moonies.

What mayhem! I processed this in a millisecond as we got closer to the bay. Screaming with excitement I abandoned my daughter and raced the remaining 50m to where the carnage was taking place. Stripping out line whilst sprinting is an art form which only GTs can make a human perform. Wading into the surf spilling over the sand bar, I double hauled the large 5/0 chartreuse deceiver into the mêlée. Instantly, the fly was knobbled by a huge GT searching for baitfish in the churned milky backwash off the sand bar. Strip striking and shouting with glee for Grace to join me, I hung on with the rod pointing straight at the fish and pulled as hard as I thought my tackle would withstand. Give a GT some line and he will show you up around the first coral head or rocky outcrop and then it's just the salty tears of defeat that remain in your memory.

I clung on to that fish, pulling hard to the left, forcing the fish to be unbalanced and use more energy, all the time in the back of my mind the thought of the many treacherous outcrops along the point. Grace was close by my side looking up at her completely fixated father peering into the

surf. Pulling hard and to the side forces fish to move in a certain direction and the bigger the fish the more determined they are to go their own way. Well in my opinion, there is only *one rule*: pull it until the fish starts to turn your way or your tackle collapses. Either way the outcome is going be the same. *If* you manage to pull *really hard* (and I mean really hard with a straight rod, very little bend in the rod, maybe a slight curve where your cork handle is) then the fish turns and you repeat the process, turning him the opposite way again. You continue this until either you land and release him or the line or tippet pops and you wave goodbye to an adversary second-to-none in the ocean. There can be no other fish with that kind of brute strength, dirty tactics and pure aggressiveness.

If you do manage to turn the fish and it charges out of the feeding zone into the reef, it's a mere second and it's over; either a shredded broken tippet or flyline is all you get as change. I hung on for as long as possible with Grace by my side, asking questions, whilst in awe of her father ranting and raving about the fish getting the better of the situation. The inevitable happened and the flyline popped from too much pressure and the GT swam off to later work out the hook jammed in the side of his mouth.

The reason this was one of my most memorable hook-ups is the fact that I lost the fish. That is the memory that haunts me. Not the many GTs I landed but the ones that got away. I can definitely remember more vividly the ones that got away than the ones I returned safely to the water. The fact that my daughter shared this experience with me enhanced it even more as we still refer to that fish with fond memories and salty shared tears of disappointment. Isn't that why we fish?

It's the memories of fish, especially the ones you only catch a glimpse of for a few seconds, that mean the most. Probably like that mermaid you once dreamed of and only met briefly. It's the same kind of passion for the ones that get away. Enjoy fishing for your mermaids!

Casting in the surf

CHAPTER 30 - MALDIVES

BEN PRETORIUS

The Maldives comprise 26 atolls and are spread in a north to south direction over a distance of 868km between latitude 7 degrees 6' 30" north and 0 degrees 42' 30" south. This offers exciting flyfishing possibilities that vary from fishing the flats, the surf zone, to bluewater. The atolls are large and unique in that there are atolls within atolls, lagoons within lagoons and it is this unusual geography that produces some of the most picture-perfect scenery imaginable. Endless brilliant white sand and coral flats, stretching as far as the eye can see, are bisected by deep, blue channels and cuttings that provide direct access to the open ocean and deep lagoons. Most of these atolls that are home to some of the most luxurious hotels on the planet do not allow fishing. However there are forgotten areas that do.

In 2008 I decided to take up the challenge of exploring what the Maldives had to offer and was accompanied by a band of experienced fly anglers on the first of two exploratory trips to these far-flung islands. Since the early exploratory trips I have hosted more than 30 groups to various

Ben Pretorius with a Maldives tank

destinations in the Maldives and have been continually impressed by the quality and abundance of the fish stocks. I am constantly researching and discovering new and better localities and we are catching more and bigger fish. I truly believe that we have only just begun to uncover what this amazing country has to offer the fly angler.

My preferred way of flyfishing is from terra firma, mainly focused on sight fishing and so I have not explored any bluewater fishing options and can be certain these too are endless. Instead I have always looked for productive flats and shore lines that offer good flyfishing potential. Initially this led me to explore the atolls to the south of Malé where I have found many big marl and sand flats as well as very productive surf fishing. These flats also offer fly anglers some of the very best triggerfishing in the world. Other species that occur on the flats and in the surf zone are the trevally species such as bluefin, GTs and yellow spotted trevally. The bluefin trevally are abundant, and fish up to 80cm fork-length have been landed, having given a very good account of themselves on a 9# rig. GTs are fairly common, but require a fair amount of stealth and good casting skills to succeed. Sightfishing to these great flyrod adversaries on the flats or in the surf and seeing them attack the fly is what dreams are made of.

Fishing for GTs in the surf zone is obviously more difficult and strenuous. Buffeting waves and rocky underfoot structure require anglers to have a good sense of humour as well as the necessary skills to be successful. Many very good fish have been caught and lost in the surf zone and despite the challenges, invariably provide anglers with many memorable experiences. To date several GTs over 100cm fork-length have been landed in the southern atolls and I have seen several fish in excess of 130cm. The day will come when one of these monster fish are landed on fly: it is only a matter of time.

In the months of February and March each year I conduct trips to atolls to the north of Malé where there are generally more sandy flats and fewer surf fishing options. As in the south, bluefin are plentiful and GTs up to 115cm have been landed. On very recent trips to the north I have discovered two new destinations that are home to numerous GTs that range in size from 60cm to 160cm. I have seen monster fish cruising well within casting distance that have ignored my 8/0 offerings with disdain. To make life even more interesting, at both these venues we have seen bonefish, triggerfish, permit and milkfish, not to mention bluefin and yellowspot kingfish.

Currently the only feasible way to fish the numerous uninhabited islands of Maldives is by way of live-aboard charter safari dhoni (traditional Maldivian vessel). In the Maldives, as opposed to other Indian Ocean atolls, there are no lengthy open ocean crossings or rough outside anchorages. Most of the sailing is done within the huge protected lagoons, some of which are in excess of 80 kilometres long. Itineraries are planned around the safest and calmest anchorages where your dhoni remains until you are ready to move on to the next fishing destination. For the more remote atolls, seaplanes or speed ferries can be used to meet the dhoni on location. In addition to the dhoni and crew, all charters come standard with a motorised skiff to transport you to and from the flats and can also be used for fishing from in deeper water. The fishing season in the Maldives runs from October to April.

GTs IN THE MALDIVES

One sunny morning on a recent trip to the northern atolls, guest Mark Meyer and I were fishing a small sandbar that is partially exposed at a low tide. On the lee of the sandbar the sand gently dropped off to a shallow, expansive flat. On the opposite side, the sand dropped off fairly sharply to a sandy shelf that was littered with coral bommies, varying in depth from three to five foot of water. This shelf extended for approximately 60 metres from the sandbar before it suddenly dropped off to 60-70 foot of bluewater. The previous day I had seen quite a few big bonefish feeding very close to the edge of the sandbar, just where the small waves were churning up the sand. I had lost two very good-size fish when the hooks pulled on their first powerful run into the deeper water and was keen to rectify the drubbing I had received.

Mark and I were patrolling the length of the sand bar when I saw a very big yellow margin trigger in amongst the bommies some 20 metres away. Two short strips of an olive clouser and the game was on as the trigger headed for the depths at an amazing pace. After several similar runs, the fish was photographed and released. Mark landed a good-sized yellow spotted trevally which was soon followed by a bonefish of about 8lb that I landed after presenting the same 2/0 olive clouser to it. I could be forgiven for feeling rather pleased with the two fish that I had landed as both qualified as the biggest of the species I had caught in the Maldives to date. Having just released the bonefish, Mark and I were discussing our bonefish tactics when I saw a huge GT cruising parallel to the same sandbar some 30 metres from us. I dropped my 9# rod and scrambled to get to my 12# rod, frantically stripping line as I ran to the far end of the bar. I managed to make a cast, leading the fish by some 10 metres, stripping the 6/0 olive semper as fast as I could.

Deepwater fight

The fish changed direction, and with an explosive burst of speed charged at the fly engulfing it in that enormous cavernous mouth. All this happened a mere ten metres from me and will be indelibly printed in my memory. With the hook firmly set, the fish turned and charged off heading for the deep blue water and beyond. It is impossible to describe in detail the speed and brute power of that first run. This is due to the fact that at this initial point in proceedings, you are definitely not in control of things whilst you are trying as best you can to manage the loose flyline that is looping out between your fingers and then having to palm a screaming reel whilst exerting as much pressure on the fish as is humanly possible, as it charges off into the blue.

After that initial blistering run of some 130 metres, the fish was well into the deep blue water when I finally managed to stop it. During the chaos of that first run, a knot had formed in the flyline as it was pulled off the beach. Under tension the knot fortunately rattled though the guide eyes closely followed by lots of 50lb backing. Aware that the knot probably weakened my flyline strength by some 50%, I remember appealing for some divine intervention as I set about trying to contain this primordial force. For the next 15 minutes the fish kept surging off, taking line, only to be stopped momentarily before surging off again. This stop/run phase of the fight is when extreme patience is required and it is very important to apply constant pressure so as to make the fish work hard for every metre of line that it takes without allowing it to rest in-between runs, constantly exerting as much pressure as you can.

Finally I began to gain back line, pumping and reeling, pumping and reeling. When the fish was some 40 metres from the shallow shelf I could feel the flyline or leader rubbing up against a coral bommie. I tried moving along the width of the sandbar to manoeuvre the fish away from potential hazards but to no avail as the fish kept heading for any structure nearest to it. Realising the possibility of losing this fish after such an arduous battle, I decided to head into the water. Initially the water was waist-deep but getting progressively deeper and I managed to climb up and stand on some of the bommies in the shallower water. I knew that if I was going to stop the fish from cutting me off, I was going to have to get out even further. This was the challenge… treading water in order to get from one bommie to the next with a huge fish pulling at the other end of my line. I had visions of being towed out into the deep but fortunately Mark had realised my predicament and swam out to anchor me from behind. With Mark as anchor-cum-drogue and attached to my back I was able to slowly manoeuvre the now exhausted fish in-between the bommies and towards the safety of the little beach.

To bring an end to this epic battle, Mark finally tailed the magnificent fish which could so easily have been lost had it not been for his quick thinking and swift response to my precarious situation. We carefully measured and photographed it and after reviving it for ten minutes, released it to fight another day. It measured 115cm fork length (30-32kg approximately). As fly anglers, we all know that to land big fish like these, we require good fortune to go our way and in this case the knot that had formed in my flyline during the first run had not given way, but was still there, now so tight and impossible to untie. It was also covered in shavings of the flyline's outer coating as it had been scuffed up against the rocks during the latter part of the fight. Sitting on the tender on our way back to the mother craft for lunch, I was keenly aware of just what a special morning's fishing I had just experienced with a very good friend. This was flyfishing at its blissful best.

CHAPTER 31 - GET FIT FOR THE FIGHT

Like all the best things in life, the more you put in, the more you get out. I have found over the last 15 years that this is certainly true of saltwater fishing, and especially GT fishing. There is nothing soft or gentle about this species and it helps hugely if the angler is physically fit. To target GTs on the fly it is often necessary to be in some of the most distant areas of the globe and this requires a certain degree of investment. You can have the top-of-the-range equipment and know exactly what you are doing, but if you physically cannot get into the environment they live in or present the fly to them then your options are limited. Even if a guide can put you into that situation on the front of a skiff and give you that shot then there is the physical aspect of the fight itself. No fishing situation with a flyrod will prepare you for how hard these things pull. On top of that you are normally in tropical heat wading amongst coral heads in the surf line, which comes with its own demands.

Those that chase GT by jigging and popping will often spend weeks in the gym training before their trip. I am not suggesting it is necessary to go to those extremes, but a basic level of fitness will massively improve your enjoyment of your trip, allow you to access areas that perhaps you would not otherwise, cover more ground and therefore increase your chances of an encounter. Think of your body as part of your equipment: it needs preparation and maintenance. This particular light bulb went off in my head on my second trip to Cosmoledo when, shall we say, I was considerably 'better covered' than on previous trips I had done. Firstly I found myself struggling in the heat as I sweated far more than I was used to and had to constantly rehydrate. I also found I was not keeping up on the long wades and as I was less alert, I missed a number of really good opportunities which I kicked myself for later. I promised myself I would not find myself in that position again.

When it came time for my first trip to Farquhar, approximately six months before I made a conscious decision to get fitter and be prepared. While I amassed new fishing tackle for the trip I came up with a few ideas that made a big difference. The secret with all exercise is to build it into your routine. If it just becomes a part of your daily life then it feels far less like an effort. I have to walk the dog every day at lunch time, so I began by trying to cover more distance in the same

amount of time by walking faster. I found that gradually over a period of weeks I could cover much longer distances in the same time-frame, and simultaneously it was becoming easier. As I walk mostly over Salisbury Plain, a large military training area, I would often see soldiers tabbing over the rough ground carrying their Bergan rucksacks which got me thinking; I could probably do that as well. I purchased an old Bergan, loaded it up with some old brochures and began to carry that on my walks. After including a couple of hills in my route I found my strength and fitness level improved quickly and the weight began to fall off. If you are going to do this it is very important to have a rucksack that has a proper frame, adjustable shoulder straps, padded hip belt and chest strap. This distributes the load properly and prevents back injury. *Do not run* while wearing this, or over time you will damage you knees and tendons.

Casting a 12# also takes some getting used to and can be physically demanding. Having a small dumbbell and practicing a casting motion with it helps to strengthening those muscles you don't use that often, as well as your wrists. Having it in your office and waving it around while you are on the telephone looks a bit odd, but will help in the long-run. I would recommend you alternate arms as well, as even though you may cast with one arm you use both to double-haul as well as your shoulders. You don't want to end up like Quasimodo, all lopsided!

If you want to take it to the next level, then some running, press-ups, pull-ups and sit-ups will never go amiss. Press-ups will strengthen your upper torso: chest, shoulders and triceps, which will help with carrying backpacks, loading boats, casting and fighting a big GT. Start by trying to achieve ten press-ups in three repetitions. As you become stronger you can build from there. The next exercise I would recommend would be sit-ups along with core exercises such as leg raises, back extensions and planks. These will aid you in the rigour of battle in the surf and help you bending your back in a fight. If you are not used to exercise or are in any doubt about how to perform these exercises safely then it is best to consult a professional trainer. Advise them on the motions of casting and let them develop a series of exercises that will prepare you. Not only is half the fun in prepping for the trip, but when you hit the flats you will really notice a difference. There is a military phrase, 'Train hard, fight easy', and this applies to GT fishing.

By the time my Farquhar trip came round that year I had dropped off a stone (14lb) in weight. I adapted to the heat faster, did not lose so much fluid, walked further without feeling it, carried larger loads, had more opportunities, cast more easily, was less fatigued and landed fish faster than on previous trips. I know this might come across as a little dramatic, but I can assure you that it makes a colossal difference. You obviously don't *have* to go to such extremes to catch GTs, but anything that can give you an edge is worth it. Time is so precious and for most people, days on the flats are a luxury. It's worth making every minute count.

The result

CHAPTER 32 - THE END OF THE LINE

Flyfishing for trevally is a privilege and should be viewed as such. Each GT I have landed over the years has been an extraordinary adventure where everything has come together in that one beautiful moment of opportunity. It is not always the case, and neither should it be, or the object of the exercise would be lost. Why do we fish for them? Landing this species on a flyrod is one of the greatest challenges that an angler can experience in saltwater. It is not about the biggest fish, or how many fish, it is about the hunt, the battle and the release. It is about the sense of achievement you feel inside when you grab that thick tail and feel the respect for a battle well fought. GTs will give their absolute all in a battle and even a small fish will pull harder than nearly every other species on the flats. Give them the respect they deserve: fight them hard and release them strong.

Most of us will have to travel thousands of miles to pinpricks of land in the middle of oceans to hunt GTs and this is half the experience. The preparation involved is like no other fly-targeted species: the extra attention that goes into every item of kit, the double-checking of every join in flylines and rigging. We know that if we turn up on the flats half-baked, any weakness will be exploited. There are very few sports that require being in the far-flung corners of the earth and I have loved every minute. You will see and experience nature in a way that those living in our normal western civilisation will never dream of and open a window on cultures that you would not normally ever have come into contact with. Why? All because of a fish. So many of us go about our daily lives living in a box of modernism, but it is vital that when you are standing on those flats in the saltwater environment these fish are found in, you take a pause and survey all around you. Don't be so single-minded in your pursuit that you miss the colourful tapestry of nature in the middle of which you are standing.

Sunset over Farquhar Atoll, Seychelles

I would urge you to treat these creatures and their environment with the utmost respect and consideration. Areas that were once prolific with trevally have sadly been plundered. It is up to us to conserve them for future generations so that they too might experience the thrill we have been lucky enough to enjoy. Flyfishing for GTs is not about numbers and I find myself increasingly shying away from those that feel the need to quantify their experience. Some of my most memorable days on the flats are when it did not all come together or even ended in total disarray. Those are the stories that are relayed around the camp fire and that keep me coming back trying to learn more. It is also vital that we look after the fragile marine eco-systems that we are moving through and try to leave as little impact of our passing as possible.

To learn, you must keep an open mind. No one out there has all the answers, but guides all have many pieces of the puzzle in their heads. If you listen to them, all those pieces of puzzle will fall into place giving you the bigger picture and you are far more likely to be successful. Having been a guide, there is nothing more frustrating than having a client who knows it all and won't listen. You should think of your guide as your team mate in this adventure. It is in their interest that you do well, so if you are receptive, they will do their best to make it happen. Even if you are a highly-experienced fisherman and you know the area well, you are not on the water on a daily basis. You will never hope to match their local knowledge of fish movement, tidal movement, reef and sand bank structure (it moves, much like a salmon river the following season after winter) and local conditions. Ask questions. Find out from your guide why they are fishing different areas at different tides, what they are hoping to see and which direction it might come from. It's all very well be taken to a spot and put on fish, but you will never develop as an angler unless you find out why they were there in the first place.

When we review the years gone by and the evolution of fishing for this particular species, it is punctuated by extraordinary people in extraordinary places. Often when a destination becomes a well-worn path rather than a simple beaten track, GTs are one of the first species to wise up. That is why those who share the obsession will never stop exploring the oceans of this world. To say that there are no areas left on the map to be discovered I don't believe to be correct. There are still true marine wildernesses out there that have had very little human contact, where GTs abound and stalk the flats. It will be the adventurous anglers who leave their footprints in the sand.

THE CONTRIBUTORS

When I embarked on this book, it was of paramount importance that it was to be inclusive. The goal for it was to become a resource of collective knowledge from the foremost people in the field who share a passion for this species. To that end I would like to thank all of those who contributed and the overwhelming enthusiasm the subject generated. All the guides are masters of their craft and the following biographies recognise their achievements.

TIM BABICH

Fishing has been Tim's lifelong passion, having been exposed to flyfishing at the very tender age of six. He has since made it his quest to pursue flyfishing as his life and career. Tim achieved numerous flyfishing qualifications including REFFIS Guide and Instructor (UK) before joining the FlyCastaway team in 2006. He has also represented his country at two freshwater world flyfishing championships in Europe. In addition to his extensive all-round angling knowledge and experience in South Africa, Tim has fished in Kenya, Mozambique, Swaziland, Zimbabwe, Seychelles, Mauritius, Zambia, Namibia, Gabon, Europe and the Amazon.

Since joining Flycastaway he has been exposed to the best GT fisheries in the world with Cosmoledo, Providence, Astove, Farquhar, Assumption and St Brandon's under his belt and has probably seen the business-end of a GT more often than most people around. He became obsessed with guiding for GTs on fly from the day he stepped onto the flats and has made it his mission to get a better understanding of this awesome predator. He is currently head guide/partner of FlyCastaway and heads up the company's operations on Farquhar, St Brandon's and Providence. He gets immense satisfaction in sharing his knowledge and passion for fishing and the environment he works in with his guests.

JAMES CHRISTMAS

James' earliest memories are of fishing the estuaries of the Eastern Cape with his father. A move north to the trout-rich farmlands of the Kwazulu Natal Midlands soon defined his path. He became solely obsessed with the lore of flyfishing from the age of seven. Tying his own flies from the age of eight, he spent every available hour exploring the wild trout streams and numerous stillwaters around South Africa. After a brief attempt at a conventional life, he abandoned such nonsense to work in flyfishing. From guiding and teaching flyfishing to running an outfitter, managing trout waters, working in a trout hatchery, to starting the first commercial flyfishing club in South Africa, he has spent time developing knowledge and experience over basically every facet of the flyfishing industry. James ran his own flytying factory where he helped develop the natural skills of ten Zulu people into expert fly tiers for four years before making his way over to the magical islands of the Seychelles.

James has spent the last seven years guiding some of the premier flats destinations such as Alphonse, Farquhar, Providence as well as completing three tours to the ultimate bonefish destination of St Brandon's Atoll off Mauritius. James has a number of unique and internationally successful fly patterns to his credit, developed during his six seasons on Alphonse Atoll. He has travelled extensively to the likes of the ASR in the Kola Peninsula in Russia, to the flats of Aitutaki in the Cook Islands. His love of trout fishing has seen him make regular visits to the fabled waters of New Zealand's South and North islands. He is equally at home flinging tiny dries on tiny fly rods as he is blasting big nasties into the deep blue. He admits though that his happy place is playing chess with the monster 'geets' of his favourite flats whilst trying to line up a guest for the perfect cast.

He believes that all paths in fishing eventually lead to the pinnacle that is flyfishing and as a flyfisher, you cannot ignore the many threats to conservation whether in the ocean or in the wilderness. James believes it is the keen sense of observation that is inevitable from spending time with a fly rod in hand, that will eventually gnaw through even the toughest barriers to shine a light on the many challenges facing the creatures and eco-systems of our wild spaces.

ANDY COETZEE

A verbatim quote from Andy's identical twin brother, Mark, whilst standing in the surf at Rocktail Bay, Maputaland in 1986. 'How do you make it look so effortless, throwing a full line in pounding surf: it's like beach ballet.' Andy Coetzee was one of the pioneers of saltwater flyfishing for GTs in the early 1980s. Living in a remote part of northern Zululand known as

Maputaland, he spent countless years developing and testing new methods and techniques whilst endeavouring to land large GTs from the surf zone of the Indian ocean. Andy was instrumental in developing the surf stripping basket, using intermediate lines and casting gigantic popping heads attached to large Deceivers and Flashy profile flies on #12 weight rigs.

As field editor for a monthly flyfishing magazine *The Complete Flyfisherman* he wrote countless articles on techniques, trevally species and destinations of the far northern regions of South Africa and Mozambique. He was the owner of a flyfishing shop, The Flyshop, for a few years but it was too far from the sea so he let his partner continue in the shop whilst he pursued GTs in Mozambique, Seychelles, Madagascar and Maldives. He was one of the few guides offering a service in South Africa and subsequently hosted flyfishing clinics/retreats on the Mozambique islands and was instrumental in developing the Seychelles outer islands flyfishing destinations Alphonse, St Josephs and Cosmoledo, exploring these islands in the late 1990s. This frenetic, rabid obsession of pursuing GTs in the surf took its toll on his married life and eventually his now ex-wife posed the dreaded ultimatum 'Choose me or fishing'. A later book published with the title *Fishing Yourself Single* says it all.

MATTHIEU COSSON

Matthieu picked up a flyrod at the age of 15, targeting the species available around his home town of Epinal. From trout to pike, European barbel to grayling and Atlantic salmon to seatrout, Matthieu has an impressive array of freshwater flyfishing techniques under his belt. After leaving his job as a pharmaceuticals expert and moving to Brittany in 2004, Matthieu worked full time as an assistant editor and photographer for the (now defunct) French magazine *Plaisirs de la Pêche*. His travels for the magazine took him to over a dozen countries with both fresh and saltwater fishing. In 2006, Matthieu made his way to Seychelles having received a text message from a friend from Belgium, asking him to guide some friends on a trip to Cosmoledo. Since then, Matthieu has guided and visited almost all of the outer islands and atolls of the Seychelles: Aldabra, African Banks, Alphonse, Assumption, Astove, Bijoutier, Cosmoledo, Desroches, Farquhar, L.D.P. Shoal, Poivre, Providence, Remire island, Remire Bank, Saint-François, Saint-Joseph, Saint-Pierre, Sand Key.

His methodical approach to successful freshwater fishing has been applied to guiding in saltwater as well. He is comfortable pursuing bumphead parrotfish and GT on the flats, bluewater fishing for sailfish and milkfish or dredging for dogtooth tuna and colourful groupers – preferably all in the same day. Now 41, Matthieu is one of the very few guides to possess such an extensive knowledge of Seychellois water and is only the second International Game Fish Association (IGFA) official representative for Seychelles. Having spent more than nine years guiding these remote outer islands, Matthieu is giving back, helping the NGO Island Conservation Society as much as he can. In 2011-2012, he has participated in the first large bonefish DNA study, carried out by the Bonefish and Tarpon Trust and Island Conservation Society Seychelles and continues to guide for Flycastaway on Farquhar, Providence and St Brandon's atolls.

WAYNE HASLEAU

Wayne has been flyfishing since he was seven years old and is a qualified and experienced fisheries technician with many years working in that field in his native South Africa. He is the longest-serving guide on Alphonse Island in the Seychelles and has been guiding seasons there since 2000. Wayne has been involved with research, development and conservation aspects of this fishery during his tenure and his main passion is flyfishing for milkfish which he pioneered in early 2002. He has come to GT fishing rather late as his focus was always on milkfish, triggerfish, permit and bonefish. In recent years, Wayne has guided at both Astove and Cosmoledo atolls and admits that he is now a confirmed GT junkie.

Wayne has developed a number of fly patterns specifically for GTs including the GT Stripping Crab, Needlefish Fly and more recently the baitfish pattern for GTs named after his close friend and fellow guide, Serge Samson, called simply 'The Serge Wrasse'. His newest GT pattern, the Cozmo-Critta is a mantis shrimp imitation. Fellow guide James Christmas developed a fabulous GT popper called the NYAP (Not Your Average Popper) a number of years ago which Wayne had the pleasure of naming for James. Wayne remains committed to the protection and conservation of wild fish resources, specifically in the Seychelles and, based on Alphonse, he intends to be involved for many years to come.

MIKE HENNESSEY

Mike is originally from California and arrived in Hawaii when he was just six years old. He grew up fishing and diving with his father in Kaneohe Bay, Oahu. It was there he first came into contact with Hawaii's monster bonefish, catching them on strips of hot dog at family BBQs. He caught his first striped marlin at the age of 10 fishing in Cabo San Lucas with his father and although the experience touched his soul and gave him a passion for offshore fishing, he also adored flyfishing for trout in the high Sierras which he still does to this day. Mike has lived, fished and guided from Cabo San Lucas to Newport Beach, California. After earning his 100-ton master's license in Oahu, Hawaii, Mike headed to Costa Rica, where he managed Cabo Matapalo Sportfishing.

Since then he has fished and guided in Fiji, Panama, Slovenia, Alaska, Costa Rica, Peru, Molokai, Palmyra Atoll, Christmas Island, Tahiti, Mexico, Florida, Nicaragua, Australia, New Zealand, Micronesia, and Indonesia. In that time he has absorbed local techniques while adding new-age methods to improve his own skills as a professional guide. Now based in Oahu, Mike and his team of guides have become specialists in hunting the giant bonefish, golden and giant trevally that frequent the flats there. Mike works with the O'io Tagging Program to gather vital information of the life-cycles and movements of the resident bonefish populations and to aid the sustainable management of the island's marine resources.

BRANDON KING

Brandon has been fishing for as long as he can remember and was first introduced to flyfishing at the age of 13 by his great-uncle whilst on a family holiday in Newfoundland fishing the local streams for brook trout. This is where his passion grew and his dream of becoming a guide took shape. At 19 his dream became a reality and he started his first guiding job in Mozambique, fishing both bluewater and inshore mangrove systems. This led him to Zambia where he guided on the Upper Zambezi targeting tigerfish on both fly and conventional gear. His love of saltwater and flyfishing eventually landed him one of the most sought-after guiding positions in the world, on Alphonse Island in the Seychelles, where he worked for 3 years. Keen to expand his horizons, he moved on to start his own fishing operation in Madagascar, targeting sailfish, marlin and giant trevally among other species.

Brandon has travelled and fished around the world searching for the next undiscovered flyfishing destination, from Australia where he targeted black marlin, queen fish, permit and golden trevally to Cuba chasing tarpon, snook and permit. His travels have taken him to Scotland for salmon where he was involved in the filming of *Once in your Life Time* a story of three anglers from around the world and their journey fishing for salmon and trout in the hills of Scotland. Recent summers have been spent exploring the Test, Dee and Kennet in the UK chasing wild brown trout and a unique trip to Slovenia had him seeking the elusive marble trout.

Brandon finally settled in Oman to start his latest flyfishing operation, Arabian Fly Sportfishing which operates in multiple destinations along the Omani coastline, offering inshore and offshore fly and conventional fishing in pursuit of Indo-Pacific permit, trevally species (giant, golden, yellow spot), bluefish, milkfish and queenfish. Offshore, billfish, dorado and tuna add to an already impressive species list.

GERHARD LAUBSCHER

Gerhard has been flyfishing since the age of 13 and started guiding after finishing school in 1994, before heading off to the University of Pretoria where he studied information science, psychology and publishing. After graduating, Gerhard decided to pursue his passion for the fishing industry and his saltwater fishing and guiding has taken him to just about every atoll and archipelago in the Indian Ocean. He was an instrumental part of the first exploratory trips to the remote outer atolls of the Seychelles and Mauritius, and in establishing these fisheries in the international flyfishing circuit. He fished extensively both the east and west coasts of Africa and his focus on Southern Africa's indigenous freshwater species such as tigerfish and yellowfish has made him a forerunner in these fields. Over the years he has fished all over Africa, Patagonia and South America, Central and North America as well as Russia and Australasia.

He has also led exploratory expeditions to other destinations in West Africa focusing on tarpon in particular. He is an accomplished fly tier and has designed numerous freshwater and saltwater fly patterns that are used all over the world today. Over the years, conservation of our natural resources has become one of Gerhard's primary objectives and he was instrumental in raising funds for, and creating, several conservation and research programs studying a variety of Africa's indigenous species. Gerhard is the Chief Executive of FlyCastaway, a South African-based guiding outfitter specialising in Indian Ocean and African destinations with their main destinations being Providence and Farquhar atolls in the Seychelles and St Brandon's Atoll in Mauritius.

JAKO LUCAS

Born and raised in Johannesburg, South Africa, Jako followed in the footsteps of his father and his grandfather and having completed University took the decision to move to the UK. Aiming to turn his passion for fishing into a career, Jako joined the team at Farlows of Pall Mall and its sister company, Sportfish, before leaving for warmer climes in January 2006. Jako has continued to guide full time, his spell in the Seychelles guiding in saltwater taking him south to the outer atolls of Cosmoledo, Providence, Astove, Assumption, Farquhar, Alphonse, St Francois and further south to Mauritian waters and St Brandon's atoll. Guiding freshwater has taken him from the Zambezi in pursuit of tigerfish to the Vaal River in South Africa in search of its indigenous smallmouth and largemouth yellowfish. Norway, with its countless fjords, lured him to guide clients pursuing Atlantic salmon and from there to Mongolia in pursuit of taimen.

For Jako, it hasn't mattered how many different fish species he has caught, the one that has captured his heart is the notoriously ill-tempered giant trevally. In his early stages of guiding, he couldn't have dreamt that his time on the flats would see his clients land close to 50 GTs in half a day, with 4,500 GTs landed overall. Never one to stand still, Jako started to combine his guiding with his love of photography and subsequently on to videography, a marriage that led him to set up Cpt Jack Films. He has, over the course of the last two years, won 3 awards for his short film, *Gangsters of the Flat*, two being the prestigious Drake Magazine Film Awards. At the time of writing, Jako's film *320* is doing the rounds across the USA on the Flyfishing Film Tour.

DAMON OLSEN

Damon Olsen was raised in Brisbane, and spent his early childhood beach fishing, camping and generally being outdoors with his parents and sister. Growing up, family holidays were spent at Hervey Bay, fishing the bay for mackerel, tuna and many other sportfish. He was a member of the Brisbane Sportfishing Club, and Sunshine Coast Gamefishing club, holding many light tackle and flyfishing records.

Damon qualified as a civil engineer, and was fortunate to have time whilst at university to fish the local Sunshine Coast and Hervey Bay waters and hone his skills catching sailfish and black marlin. His time at University coincided with one of the best runs of billfish ever recorded in Australian waters, and he skippered the family's small boat to tag and release the record number of billfish in Australian water for two years in a row, tagging in excess of 400 billfish each year. The prolific fishery provided a steep learning curve and skills that would have taken much longer to develop elsewhere were refined in short time.

After leaving University and working as an engineer for 18 months, Damon realised that his passion to start a charter operation and explore the Coral Sea and Great Barrier Reef was something that he simply had to do. This started with refurbishing a small 'mini mothership' with his father and running a successful operation out of Hervey Bay for several years, before embarking on project-managing the build of the 80ft Odyssey II. The charter operation at Fraser Island proved that the concept was good, and the interest from anglers in being part of a mothership operation exploring the outer Coral Sea and remote far northern Great Barrier Reef has simply grown. The Nomad Sportfishing operation today takes anglers from around the world to some of the world's most prolific bluewater sportfishing areas. The remote nature of the operation and logistical challenges involved have seen Nomad Sportfishing pioneer an operation that remains unmatched to this day and they are still currently the only operators to fish in 80% of the waters they operate in.

TIM PASK

Tim's grandfather worked for Bronson Reels (located in Bronson, Michigan and long since out of business), but he can still remember him giving him his first flyrod and reel when he was 11. Not much double-hauling was happening, but as far as the bluegills were concerned, he was Darth Vader and the Force was strong within him. Decades passed, and Tim's passion for all things outdoors continued to grow. But in 1995 everything changed forever. That was the year Tim found himself on the flats of Christmas Island having his first encounter with a giant trevally. Under-geared and overwhelmed, would best describe that first week on the saltwater flats, but that first encounter ignited a passion that all but consumed him for years to come.

In those early days nothing seemed good enough. Dacron backing broke, flylines virtually melted in the heat, the bimini twist sounded more like a dance move than a knot, and hooks straightened like they were made from rubber. Yet he managed to land the occasional GT. Nothing over 40 pounds seemed humanly possible then, but as the tackle improved and Tim's knowledge increased, the game began to change in his favour, and then the GTs began to fall.

Tim is proud to have released every single giant trevally he's ever caught, and plans to continue that practice going forward. He's said on more than one occasion that there's not much that compares with landing a huge GT. The fight is unbelievable, but once you've won the battle, the GT actually seems to surrender. It's almost unbelievable to cradle a huge GT in your arms and then to watch it slowly swim away and survive to fight another day.

GRAHAM POLLARD

Graham was born in Zimbabwe and grew up in Zambia, Portugal and Mozambique. His love of fishing began at an early age with trips to the Lower Zambezi with his father, fishing for the spectacular tigerfish. When his family moved to Maputo in 1992 at the end of the war in Mozambique, Graham spent every school holiday and spare moment fishing the waters around Inhaca Island.

He was warded a B.Sc in Zoology and Ocean & Atmosphere Science at University of Cape Town which seemed like the perfect qualification to become a fishing guide. His first guiding job was in Zambia's Barotse flood plains hunting for his old foe, the tigerfish. From here he returned to Mozambique and spent time guiding clients in the north of the country at the Quirimbas Archipelago before heading south to the Bazaruto Archipelago where he had the good fortune of working under Andrew Parsons before taking over his fishing business there.

Graham is now based in southern Mozambique, not far from Inhaca Island, where he and his wife run a private villa. Graham guides private clients part time and has had the good fortune of having spent time fishing all over the world and guiding in Zambia, Mexico, Seychelles and the Maldives.

BEN PRETORIUS

During December 1991 whilst fishing with live bait from a boat on an Eastern Cape estuary, Ben was inspired by the skill and subtlety demonstrated by two young anglers flyfishing from the bank nearby on that day. Back home, with the assistance of limited literature, friends, acquaintances, a flycasting clinic with Jack Blackman and a lot of dogged determination, he learnt how to cast – and so began his passion for flyfishing. In the hours he and Jack Blackman spent discussing the importance of a good cast in the pursuit of flyfishing, they decided to put their passion, skills and experience together and developed their own practical workshop to help others improve their casting. This led to the launch of the Ufudu Flyfishing Experience, a mobile tented camp accommodating guests at Kosi Bay (on the Maputaland north coast) and the Mtentu river mouth (on the Wild Coast of the eastern Cape).

Whilst at Kosi Bay, Ben became obsessed with the challenge of landing on fly the metre-plus (20kg) GTs that were at home in the surf of that reef-strewn and rugged coastline. His first success came in the form of a 104cm fish which gave him plenty of inspiration to refine the tackle set-up. By way of reference, approximately 13 of these metre-plus fish have been landed from the South African rock and surf zone, with the biggest measuring 118cm. In 2003 Pam and Ben moved to Kloof where they set up their office, a flycasting academy, a small fly tying factory and a flyfishing shop. Among some of the very practical innovations that have resulted from Ben's immersion in the sport are the waist bag, a personal floatation device, a flyline spooler, a GT flyline for local conditions, a spare rod clip, reel dust covers and a heat-shrink rod grip.

An avid conservationist, a strict catch-and-release practitioner, Ben has been described as being somewhat dogmatic about only fishing from terra firma and practising sight fishing where and whenever possible and he is very comfortable with these references. When he is not hosting trips to the Maldives and other parts of South Africa, Ben regularly conducts saltwater workshops, gives flycasting lessons, oversees the production of increasingly more effective and popular flies, deals with the paperwork and occasionally writes articles for various publications. At the ripe young age of 65, Ben is still obsessed with sight casting a fly to big GTs from terra firma and is increasingly passionate about passing this obsession on to whoever is interested.

KEITH ROSE-INNES

Born and brought up in South Africa, Keith's fishing and guiding portfolio is extensive, with over 30 years flyfishing experience of which he has spent 19 years guiding. He has been flyfishing his entire life and following in the footsteps of his Scottish grandfather, Harry Stewarts, he has travelled around the globe in the hunt for gamefish. His guiding portfolio extends to over 22 countries and includes 19 years exploring, pioneering, promoting and establishing the remote atolls of the Seychelles now firmly on the world's flyfishing map. He was among the first to flyfish and guide trips to the remote southern atolls of the Seychelles and his extensive experience in the Indian Ocean has seen him become one of the most experienced GT guides and flyfishermen around, with over 5,200 client-caught GTs. Keith has been at the forefront of developing techniques on how to catch Indian Ocean species initially viewed as uncatchable and is credited for successfully working out how to catch bumphead parrotfish on fly.

His hard GT fighting technique is unique and has been adopted by many guides and anglers over the years. In doing so Keith has worked alongside various flyrod, flyline, hook, braid, clothing and reel companies developing a standard of tackle, gear and rigging that can survive the extremes associated with casting big flies and fighting explosive gamefish in the tropics. Keith is a gameboat Captain and it's his in-depth knowledge of all different facets of fishing which has helped him become one of the leading GT specialists. His experience extends further than the salt as he spent four years as head guide on the Ponoi River in Russia fishing for Atlantic salmon. Keith is the Managing Director and one of the founding members of Alphonse Fishing Company, one of the biggest flyfishing operations in the world, with 5 different island destinations, namely Alphonse Island, Astove Atoll, Desroches Island, Cosmoledo Atoll and Poivre Atoll.

SERGE SAMSON

In the same way that cold and beer, or fish and chips, go together, so do Serge Samson and GTs. Born and raised in the Seychelles, Serge has been guiding clients in the saltwater for over 15 years. Of that, he guided on Alphonse for 14 years, starting off helping out and being thrown in the deep end and given a week to learn how to guide, a challenge to which he rose admirably. At a time when GTs were not considered a primary target, he quickly gained a reputation for finding and catching these majestic fish. It's a telling observation that throughout his tenure on Alphonse, he was universally respected by his fellow guides, and trainees quickly found themselves in awe of the 'rasta's' uncanny ability to find fish. When asked how and why he went to Alphonse in the first instance, Serge replies (imagine you are a Seychellois Rastafarian to get the best effect) 'Because my friend, he said to me, he knows a man who is saying come to Alphonse to work. So I said OK and I went.' It was as simple as that.

Some plot a life course whilst others go where opportunity and talent take them and Serge conforms to the latter. Having spent nearly two decades on the flats of Alphonse, St Francois, Astove and Cosmoledo watching GTs and learning their habits, understanding how and why they respond – or don't – to various stimuli in a variety of environments, his reputation as 'the GT man' is indisputable. Were you to ask Serge how many GTs he has guided his clients to, he'd shake his head and say 'many, yah, many'. A more modest man about his inherent skill in finding and understanding GTs, you could not hope to find. This rare quality is sometimes unsettling for expectant clients when they are excitedly talking about catching GTs and getting a smiling 'we try' as a reply. Although a man of few words, and those seldom include 'no' if the question involves a takamaka, Serge is happiest shouting 'Strip, strip, strip' with the occasional cutting observation thrown in...'Too short, too short, you strip like a girl'.

Serge continues to guide in the Seychelles and the outer atolls, currently working for a private charter company out of Mahé, enjoying being able to spend time with his wife Gemma, daughter and son. He continues to love what he does, enjoying meeting and guiding new guests and taking incredible pleasure from being part of their GT challenge and experience.

LUKE WYRSTA

Luke was born in Sydney, Australia in 1985 and by four years of age, his appreciation of the peaceful pastime was already budding. His love of 'wetting a line' was predominantly nurtured by his grandmother, although his grandfather and father played a large part in fostering his enthusiasm. Endless days were spent fishing for estuary species on the tranquil Georges River and in Port Hacking. By the age of 16 his thirst for fishing knowledge and experience was insatiable. Luke's acquaintance with the 'long wand' was already made with seasonal trips to the Snowy Mountains targeting brown trout. Regular family holidays to south-east Queensland were an opportunity to target new species and eventually he was exposed to what would become his favourite species: GTs. Luke began targeting the species seriously in 2004 using some of the first primitive equipment to reach Australian shores from Japan. Most were land-based expeditions in Cairns, north Queensland and Exmouth, Western Australia. Over the following three years Luke managed to fish the Great Barrier Reef and Fraser Island.

Luke began working for Shimano Australia under the auspices of the much-revered John Dunphy, a man for whom Luke had tremendous respect and gratitude. Early trips included visits to Fiji and the Gilbert Islands, West Kiribati and he has had the honour of fishing with Kenzaburo

Fukui in Amami and Tokara, Japan, and made multiple trips with New Caledonia pioneers David and Rudy Boue-Mandil. He fished Socotra, Yemen before its secrets were exposed to the world and fished Southern Oman in its booming years. Regular trips continued to the Great Barrier Reef, Fraser Island and Hawaii. Luke's goal is to uncover the last remaining and most remote, untouched GT popping and flycasting destinations. In 2013 Luke was credited with discovering the enormous potential of the Louisiade Archipelago, Papua New Guinea and recently in 2015 after years of hard work and dedication, succeeded in his most treasured accomplishment to date: a tremendously successful expedition to rediscover Kanton Island, Kiribati. Luke continues to work respectfully and closely with the traditional landowners in PNG and Kiribati with the hope of fulfilling his dream of guiding fly and top-water clients to unforgettable captures in a region that he, himself, has pioneered.

Mayas Dugong at anchor off Assumption Atoll, Seychelles

PHOTO CREDITS

When embarking on a project such as this, trying to find imagery to visually illustrate the words can be a serious challenge. I would like to say a huge thank you to all of those who have freely donated their images and embraced the ideas behind this book. I would like to thank in particular our staff photographer Henry Gilbey whose images grace the cover along with many chapters in between. Gerhard Laubscher allowed me free access to his image database for which I shall be forever grateful.

Aside from the contributors themselves, the others I would like to thank who have all contributed are: Alphonse Island Fishing Company, FlyCastaway, Mark Murray, Bradley Hyman, Mark Hatter, Andrew Mayo, Vadim Titovets, Christiaan Pretorius, AOS Fly Fishing through Stefan & Alex Haider, Jerry Swanson, Tim Pilcher, Tarquin Millington-Drake, Julien Lajournade, Wesley de Klerk, Ralph Meyer-Rust, Francois Botha, Joern Heiner, Roby Bresson, Nick Clewlow, Matt Harris, James Christmas, John Wolstenholme, Ian Hodge, Ty Pollock, Michael Novak and the many others who made this project possible.

BIBLIOGRAPHY

Van der Elst, Rudy; Peter Borchert (Ed.) (1994) *A Guide to the Common Sea Fishes of Southern Africa* New Holland Publishers p142 ISBN 1-868253-94-5

Froese, Rainer and Pauly, Daniel, eds. (2009) *Caranx ignobilis* in FishBase September 2009 version

Smith-Vaniz, W. (1999) Carangidae. In Carpenter, K.E. & Niem, V.H. *The Living Marine Resources of the Western Central Pacific Vol. 4: Bony Fishes, Part 2 (Mugilidae to Carangidae)* (PDF). FAO species identification guide for fishery purposes. Rome: FAO pp. 2659-2757 ISBN 9-251043-01-9

Hutchins, B; Swainston, R. (1986) *Sea Fishes of Southern Australia: Complete Field Guide for Anglers and Divers* Melbourne: Swainston Publishing. p.187. ISBN 1-862526-61-3

Honebrink, Randy R. (2000) *A review of the biology of the family Carangidae, with emphasis on species found in Hawaiian waters* (PDF). DAR Technical Report (Honolulu: Department of Land and Natural Resources). 20-01: 1–43. Retrieved 2009-05-11

Rick Gaffney and Associates, Inc. (2000) *Evaluation of the status of the recreational fishery for ulua in Hawai'i, and recommendations for future management* (PDF). Division of Aquatic Resources Technical Report (Department of Land and Natural Resources, Hawaii). 20-02: 1–42. Retrieved 2009-09-14

Lin, Pai-Lei; Shao, Kwang-Tsao (1999). *A Review of the Carangid Fishes (Family Carangidae) from Taiwan with Descriptions of Four New Records Zoological Studies* 38 (1): 33–68

Smith-Vaniz, W (1999). Carangidae. In Carpenter, K.E. & Niem, V.H. *The living marine resources of the Western Central Pacific Vol 4. Bony fishes part 2 (Mugilidae to Carangidae)* (PDF). FAO species identification guide for fishery purposes. Rome: FAO. pp. 2659–2757. ISBN 9-251043-01-9

Talbot, FH; Williams, F. (1956) *Sexual colour differences in Caranx ignobilis (Forsk.)* Nature 178 (4539): 934–5. doi:10.1038/178934a0.PMID 13369587

Sudekum, AE; Parrish, JD; Radtke, RL; Ralston, S (1991) *Life History and Ecology of Large Jacks in Undisturbed, Shallow, Oceanic Communities* (PDF) Fishery Bulletin 89 (3): 493–513. Retrieved 2009-09-14

Potts, GW (1981) *Behavioural interactions between the Carangidae (Pisces) and their prey on the fore-reef slope of Aldabra, with notes on other predators* Journal of Zoology 195 (3): 385–404. doi:10.1111/j.1469-7998.1981.tb03472.x

Williams, F (1965) *Further notes on the biology of the East African pelagic fishes of the Families Carangidae and Sphyraenidae* Journal of East African Agriculture and Forestry 31: 141–168

Smith, GC, Parrish, JD (2002). Estuaries as *Nurseries for the Jacks Caranx ignobilis and Caranx melampygus (Carangidae) in Hawaii* Estuarine, Coastal and Shelf Science 55 (3): 347–359. doi:10.1006/ecss.2001.0909

Major, PF (1978) *Predator-prey interactions in two schooling fishes, Caranx ignobilis and Stolephorus purpureous* Animal Behaviour 26 (3): 760–777. doi:10.1016/0003-3472(78)90142-2

Kauffman, Randal *Bonefishing!* Western Fisherman's Press in 2000, ISBN 1-885212-13-5

Combs, Trey *Bluewater Flyfishing* Lyons & Burford, 1995 ISBN 1-558213-31-7